The Heart of Soul

An Africentric Approach To Psycho-spiritual Wholeness: Volume I

John L. Bolling, M.D.

A Manual of the Rites-Of-Passage to A Soul-Centered Worldview

Bloomington, IN  Milton Keynes, UK

authorHOUSE®

AuthorHouse™
1663 Liberty Drive, Suite 200
Bloomington, IN 47403
www.authorhouse.com
Phone: 1-800-839-8640

AuthorHouse™ *UK Ltd.*
500 Avebury Boulevard
Central Milton Keynes, MK9 2BE
www.authorhouse.co.uk
Phone: 08001974150

First published by AuthorHouse 4/14/2008

ISBN: 978-1-4259-9762-5 (sc)

Library of Congress Control Number: 2007901383

Printed in the United States of America
Bloomington, Indiana

This book is printed on acid-free paper.

Artwork: *David Jones*
                       Jemesi Obanjoko
Photography: *Richard Tanco*
                       John L. Bolling

To Black Children of Yesterday, Today and Tomorrow
You are the dreams of yesterday which change has
thrust abruptly into today to unfold the future
of a million tomorrows.

FOR NOTES
Insights, Reflections, Self-Observations

TABLE OF CONTENTS

PREFACE:

This book has grown out of many years of research, introspection, travel, observation and inner spiritual work. It has evolved out of a growing and ever unfolding need to understand the culture of Soul and how it applies to human growth and maturation. While I believe that nothing truly original can be said, I have attempted to give my own unique and creative interpretation to the Soul from an Africentric perspective. The Soul, from this perspective has seldom been written about in books since most of the culture of Soul has been passed on non-verbally and by oral tradition.

It has not been my attempt to create a new theory about the Soul, but rather to label, document and expand those structures that already exist as retentions of Soul culture. By so doing, the culture of Soul can lend wholeness, meaning, purpose and unity to our daily lives during these times of great transition and transformation. The culture of Soul can assist us at the personal, family and social levels with meaningful values and behaviors as we strive to uplift and heal ourselves.

It has always distressed me greatly that the traditional psychological models that are supposed to be about the study of the Soul (psyche = soul; -ology = study of) have completely deleted the Soul. This gross and obvious deletion results in a one-sided, intellectual psychology which is not only non-healing to those people and cultures that depend upon a worldview of "Soul", but is detrimental to their, as well as, the national character development. With the Heart of Soul deleted, the heart of human development and maturation is missing.

As a consequence of the deletion of this heart of Soul from current Western psychological models, I personally witnessed throughout my psychiatric training the mis-application of psychiatry to mis-label and mis-manage many experiences in non-mainstream, non-European groups. For instance, one of the frequent presenting complaints of many of the children, both African-American and African-Caribbean, was the experience of an inner voice telling them things to do. Often this inner voice was accompanied by visual experiences of deceased relatives such as grandparents or other departed loved ones.

When I would defend these experiences against the mislabeling process by explaining these as phenomena of the culture of Soul, my supervisors would frequently ask, "What is this culture of Soul that you are speaking about?". Often I would be admonished to not speak of the Soul in the sacred halls of science since it was nebulous and could not be proven and validated by fact and measurement. My persistent attempts to explain the cultural experiences of these children resulted in a remark by one of my immediate supervisors that started me on my Journey Into The Self—the search for the Soul. After I gave my usual defense of these intuitive phenomena, she said "this culture of Soul that you speak of is nothing more than what we see in your sports, in your music, in your dance but when it comes to explaining how this culture of Soul relates to personality development, you are not able to tell us—therefore there is nothing." She concluded in her perfectly rational and scientific manner that therefore "you know that you really don't have any more culture than that which we Europeans have given to you."

This remark was the stimulus to set me thinking and searching for the missing documentation, theory, beliefs, and techniques of the Soul-Centered worldview. In producing this book, I have drawn from many sources and acknowledge the many gaps and redundances in presenting a unified Soul-Centered worldview. I have attempted to present some of the key issues at the Heart of Soul that apply to everyday growth and maturation. In many cases, the seeming repetitions in the book are unavoidable and in other cases, they are intentional. Like DNA which repeats itself throughout each cell of the body, certain themes and terms are repeated throughout each chapter to serve as the organic unity central to a Soul-Centered worldview.

I realize that there are shortcomings in the presentation and have planned to address some of these in the forth coming series of books on the topic of Soul-Centered Healing.

As I searched for the heart of this Soul-Centered worldview, it became apparent to me that it was a complex, multi-dimensional, multi-axial, interconnecting reality which is the mandala of the Self. It also became aware to me that it would be impossible to attempt to describe this complex reality in the lineal language structure which characterizes our present reality. I have therefore included periodic illustrations with the hope that a picture will be worth a thousand words.

The spiritual, Soul-Centered worldview (African, Asian, Indian, etc) differs from the material worldview (European, Euro-American). The two exist on different planes of reality. In the material worldview, the concrete world of seen and felt objects is viewed as being the causation and motivation for life and reality. The material worldview exists on a lineal, rational, logical, horizontal, material plane and can best be understood in a language structure which describes this material, one-dimensional reality.

The spiritual worldview of African and Eastern cultures primarily expouses the unseen invisible forces of the Soul—the Great Mother, the Earth Mother, the "Dark Mother"—"The Black Goddess". The Soul as "Mother Africa Within" is the spiritual world which serves as the heart, source, center, the intelligent causation and motivation for life and reality. Mother Africa is the Mother Root of Soul.

The Soul exists as a multi-axial wheel. A mandala, which is usually shown as a complex geometrical design of wheels-within-a-wheel, would be a good example of a model of the Soul with its multi-tiered levels of symbolism and interrelated planes. The central coordinate of the mandala is the vertical axis of reality. The Soul can best be understood in a language structure which describes this invisible, multi-axial, multi-layered reality. From an Africentric viewpoint, it is this invisible-spiritual realm of the Dark Mother which is as real or more real than the lineal, material, conscious reality. It is within the mantle of the Dark Mother that the universe and suprauniverses are suspended. She represents the VOID, the Black Space—the GROUND of NO-THING in which all time and substance is embedded and out of which they are born. She represents the dark space of death to which all time and substance returns. She represents a multi-tiered, complex reality which is different from the ego-centered, material-centered reality of Western culture. Ideally we should be able to experience many different levels of both realities in their complex, multi-peeling existence at once without losing site of the present moment. In the highest realms of consciousness one could expect to perhaps experience all levels at once (synesthesia) without losing focus of the present moment.

The Soul as the archetypal symbol of the "Dark Feminine" or "Black Goddess" is herein introduced and hopefully validated as the missing and repressed element in psychology and philosophy. The re-introduction of this element will allow for the synthesis and integration of two otherwise disparate and ofttimes opposing worldviews – Africentric and Eurocentric. Unless these two polar worldviews are harmonized, the American society at large is headed towards total "Chaos". Martin Luther King, Jr's. book "Where Do We Go From Here: Chaos or Community" addresses this issue of inner synthesis, integration and healing of the collective character structure of modern man as Community. In the lack of healing, both the White and Black worldviews will descend into the inevitable fragmentation and disintegration of Chaos.

The "Dark Feminine" or "Black Goddess" as archetypal symbol of the Soul, in this dual aspect of Community and Chaos, then represents both the dream and the underside of the dream—the nightmare. Community and Chaos are but wings of the Goddess Ma-at held together at the center, her Heart of Soul, with TRUTH.

The reality of the Beloved Community can only proceed as the two polar worldviews, Africentric and Eurocentric, are hooked-up, integrated into one whole associated view of reality—the reality that IS.

The Dark Mother represents that multi-axial, multi-tiered reality of invisible forces which comprises the unconscious mind or Soul. We have failed to validate this archetypal consciousness of the Dark Mother in western culture. We have continuously repressed and disowned Her. We have resisted the internalization and integration of Her Soul Forces into our conscious lives.

The Dark Mother as archetypal symbol of the Soul is a magnetico-electric, multi-tiered sheath arranged in and around our physical form as layers extending infinitesimally out into time and space—our aura. Embedded in infinitesimal space, these layers of Self are continuous with that from which they derive and with that to which they seek return and reunion—The Black Goddess.

The African worldview is a living practice of, participation with, celebration of, union with these unconscious, invisible extensions of self as Soul Forces. This is opposed to the European worldview of "thinking" and "rationalizing" about them. The language of the Soul consists of rhythm, movement, action, symbol and imagery, all of which require an **active participation**. It is hard to convey to the reader this necessary and felt sense of "participation" in these Soul Forces without suggesting that the reader do something active while reading this book.

The reader may be able to get more of a sense of participation in the Heart of Soul by performing some of those participatory ritual practices that have been preserved in Africentric, Soul-Centered culture for centuries. These practices involve doing such things, to use some examples, as bathing in certain herbs three times per week as you are reading chapter one; putting a glass of water under the head of your bed, emptying and refreshening it every friday night as you are reading chapter two; or just before starting to read the chapter on the seven-levels of the Soul, putting a flower of Jericho in a bowl of water and when it has opened, drop seven pennies into its heart and ask that the walls of resistance to going below the surface of consciousness be broken down. Further examples of participational learning from both the right and the left brain would include such Africentric practices as making certain offerings at the ocean when the reader has reached a certain point in the book or say a certain prayer to the "Opener Of The Way" as a new chapter is to be opened. Other participational rituals would include doing a certain dance with emphasis on certain body motions and rhythms in order to integrate and internalize the contents at the close of each chapter; or light a seven-day candle when enlightened usage of the material of the book is sought in its application to everyday life.

The soul, as the Dark Mother, is the invisible connection link between the various visible components of reality. The Dark Mother—Mother Africa Within—is the heart and center of psychology, reality, and being. She is that unspoken and unbroken matrix, the "prima materia", the Ground which interweaves, knits and symbolically links all the pieces together.

Just as separateness, discreteness, concreteness, difference are all valued qualities of western-material culture, similarity, association, hooked-togetherness, connectedness are all valued qualities of African and Africentric cultures. At the Heart of Soul everything is connected together as a unified Community of Oneness. This book purposefully employs several associations throughout various philosophical and psychological systems to attempt to induce in the reader a sense of this associative-symbolic, linking function of the Soul. I have intentionally employed multiple nouns linked in sequence to attempt to give a feeling of this linked-together reality of the Soul.

The writing of this book attempts to initiate the reader into an alternate view of reality which is not always found in the written word on the page, but rather through the connectedness, the hooked-togetherness and associations that are raised. In this manner the reader will be pulled below the surface of the page into a vertical reality—into the Heart of Soul—which is a complex multi-layered and multi-axial reality found within the individual Soul as it connects to the Universal Soul. The writing of this book attempts to pick up the "Aradnye threads" of the Soul which connect similar symbolic themes across time and space which manifest in various cultures which seem to have no obvious connecting relationships. In all cultures, but especially in African and Asiatic cultures, certain people and certain rituals have always served as mediums or channels for this sub-surface, invisible, multi-axial, multi-tiered, collective pool of ancestral wisdom.

During the course of this book, if each time I wanted to get the complexity of this circular multi-tied, multi-axial, self-regenerative reality of the Soul across to the reader, I could draw the uroboric symbol.

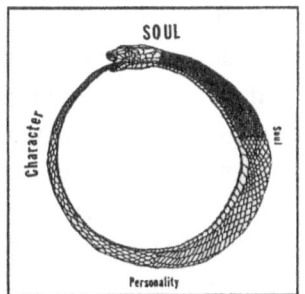 

Urobrorous

The symbol of the uroborous is a serpent swallowing its tail as it appears in the ancient symbols of many primal cultures. The repetitive drawing of this symbol throughout the book however would constitute a reversion to an earlier communicational system employed specifically for this purpose, a type of hieroglyphic writing designed to convey not one singular word or idea, but a complex system of multi-dimensional thought, action and values.

Ideally, hieroglyphics would be the perfect language in which to describe the contents and the complexities of the Soul but few people would be able to read or understand their messages. So I have settled for such constructions as a series of hooked-together nouns to convey this complex, circular, connected reality. The following is an example of such a construction which is used throughout the book to symbolize the uroboric nature of the Self, the soul-personality-ego-character-SOUL. The first small soul which is not capitalized symbolizes the natal soul incarnating to begin its learning experiences in and through the various "fields" of reality. Its lessons are incorporated into the personality and later into the character structure. The capitalized SOUL represents the perfected, regenerated, transformed aspect of Self development and maturation which signifies the balanced-integrated state of Self-Realization.

This balanced-integrated state of Self-Realization—the SOUL—represents a state of having learned and incorporated the lessons of the various sub-levels of reality—the "fields of experience" and having come to union with the SELF on the Higher Planes Of Reality. If I stopped to explain this complex idea of the soul-personality-character-SOUL each time I wanted to discuss this process I would never finish the book. Therefore I am hoping the readers will be able to follow this multi-tiered reality of the Soul when I use such hooked-together constructions as soul-personality-ego-character-SOUL.

There are other such hooked together constructions which I have not taken the time to explain in the hope that the reader will be familiar with a cross section of literature representative of the two worldviews which I attempt to synthesize in this work. Many times I employ terms from the literature of both worldviews (Africentric and Eurocentric) with which only certain readers or practitioners would have some familiarity. This practice of using terms from both worldviews are felt to be necessary as I attempted to interweave and connect the two worldviews and belief-systems. To facilitate the understanding of these terms, I have included a reference list at the end of the book, outlined by chapters.

More importantly, I have attempted to remove the focus as much as possible from my own thinking about these issues by quoting and documenting symbolic themes that serve as the connecting links between the two worldviews and which speak for themselves. I must admit that at times artistic license had to be employed to create a connecting word to bridge the two disparate worldviews when an appropriate word did not exist in the language of either worldview. If the reader is not somewhat drawn below the surface of the page into the Heart of this multi-axial, multi-tiered reality of Soul, then the purpose of the book has not succeeded.

The Western world is currently going through a rites-of-passage or a self-structuring hierarchical jump into a new reality. This book and others in the Soul-Centered Healing Series are designed to assist individuals and groups in this transition into new vistas of consciousness. Therefore the book is not intended to be read with full understanding at one or two continuous readings. Throughout the book, certain exercises are interspersed in order to shift the reader from the intellectual mode to the experiential mode. When the contents of the book become too complex, it should be put aside to be picked up at a later time. During this interim period, it would be helpful to explore some of the background references. Some might find it beneficial to skip to a section one might feel more drawn to and a section which might be more easily digested, only later to come back to the more difficult sections.

Because of the associative-symbolic linking function of the Soul, it can not be understood in the usual linear-surface approach to reality that is prized in western culture. The Soul—the Dark Mother—is a below-the-surface reality, a "background" phenomenon which organizes conscious foreground attitudes, values, behaviors and interactions. The Soul requires that one perceives and apperceives at the same time—that one "sees" reality in its fuller dimensions. This requires us to "see" and think in many dimensions at once, which is the reality of our Being and the challenge of twenty-first century humanity. The world has become too complex and hooked-together to continue to think of in our usual simplistic, separated, materialistic categories. The re-emergence of The Dark mother as the Heart of Soul and as archetypal symbol of the Beloved Community is not possible employing old mindsets.

The writing of this book is intended to point in the direction of a new reality that is just unfolding as the Beloved Community—the re-en-Souling of humanity and the world. This re-en-Souling process has progressed beyond a "dream" and is fastly becoming a reality of Universal Law—an imperative of human evolution. Since this re-en-Souling is the reality of our destiny and higher Being, It can be resisted but not stopped in Its unfoldment. Those who are within Its growth are enhanced by Its unfoldment, and those outside of Its growth are destroyed by Its unfoldment.

The book is produced with the hope of providing a foundation in Soul-Centered psychology for students of psychiatry, psychology, social work, education and other helping professionals. This foundation hopefully will provide sufficient background of the culture of Soul and the Dark Feminine to help them respond sufficiently when the question is next asked during their training process "What is this worldview of soul culture?". The book is also produced to stimulate research in a frontier of science which is the area of exploration for the new decade—the Science of the Soul.

The author is grateful to all persons who have contributed their wisdom and skills, both directly and indirectly, to bring the work from the realm of idea to the realm of reality. I would especially like to mention the special help and encouragement that I have received from people such as Elsie Delfin (Cuca), Carmen Cruz, Evelyn Edmund, Paul Dunn, George Harrison, Socorro Byron, Danny Dawson, Marta Vega, Ruth Knox, Richard Tanco, Mary Connelly , Sally Scott, Norda Dienstag, Evelyn Darrell, Dale Ellison and other unnamed persons. I am especially thankful to all of the Black and Hispanic children who have contributed indirectly though the spontaneity and sharing of their thoughts and intuitions.

I give special thanks for the editorial assistance of Louis Young and others who read this manuscript and gave helpful feedback about content and style.

FOR NOTES
Insights, Reflections, Self-Observations

FOR NOTES
Insights, Reflections, Self-Observations

CHAPTER 1:

The Soul Of Mother Africa As Sacred Mandala

The Soul of Mother Africa is a sacred Mandala as magnetic-electrical energetic forces. A mandala is a circle of balance consisting of many smaller interrelated and symmetrically arranged circles within the circle. The mandala as symbol of the Soul is a hologram. It has its own built-in mechanism to re-establish balance and harmony. The mandala forces integration when any one aspect of the whole gets too far out of balance. It calls from its deepest center—or Heart—for a return to the Source and sets in motion the forces of integration, transformation and change.

In this regards, the major principle of the Mandala is that of "Center". The organizational structure of everything from the sub-atomic to the supra-universes is a mandala and contains a center. The major movement of growth, organization, maturation and evolution is one of centering and "centroversion". Centroversion is a term used by Neuman in referring to this inner psychic call to the Center, the Source, the Heart.

While the process of centering (voluntarily choosing to find the center) depends largely on the small conscious will and Life-style issues, the act of centroversion (involuntarily being pulled to the center) depends on the greater spiritual WILL from the "yoking center"—the Heart of the Life-Track. The Life-Track is introduced

1

in this writing as that coherent system of myths, beliefs, values, practices, rituals that comprise the Collective Soul of a culture.

Therefore, everything in the universe from the sub-microscopic to the supra-universe, is an intricate system of mandalas which are interrelated, associated and forever restructuring themselves. This constant restructuring is necessary for higher efficiency and ultimate coalescing with the one Great Mandala—The Unified Field of Energy, The "Inner Community of Oneness"—The Beloved Community.

A Mandala

The archetype of the "Inner Community of Oneness", upon which this book and its theoretical model is based, draws heavily upon Martin Luther King, Jr's dream of the evolving inner "Beloved Community". Martin Luther King, Jr. like Gandhi before him, based his social movement to build the Beloved Community upon these inner Soul Forces. This Concept of the inner Beloved Community is very much an African concept having been expressed centuries ago by another great African, St. Augustine in his timeless book—The City Of God. The symbols of Community and communalism serve as the foundation of the African family and social structure. This Beloved Community is a symbol of righteousness, right relations, justice, truth, harmony, peace and love. It represents the full development of the creative potentialities of the individual and the group. This symbol of the Beloved Community also represents a re-establishment of harmony with Motor Nature and Her Soul Forces as the indwelling divinity on the earth, as well as, the cosmic planes. The Earth Mother as the Dark Goddess and Her Soul Forces are the organizing forces at the center of all things that are manifested and unmanifested. All of these Soul Forces are ultimately organized around the unity and the harmony of the evolving "Beloved Community".

Within this model of the Soul or Great Mandala, each individual is viewed as a structural and energy matrix through, and from, which flows successive Soul Force energies. This structural and energy matrix forever changes in a series of symbolic stages on the transformative journey into union with the Source. Within, the individual is a dynamic conglomerate of energy complexes and structural sub-systems arranged in a hierarchical fashion. Each sub-system set or template may be viewed as a mandala with a center. These template centers organize themselves into systems for the harmonious contribution to the central "Life Force" of the individual and collective group as infra, supra and mega-systems of organization, ad infinitum.

The center of each Mandala is connected to, contributed to by, and receives from, successive infra and supra-centers of Vital Force. Each Mandalic (soul force) energy system, herein referred to as Mandala-Imago-Symbolic-Energy-System-Complexes (M.I.S.E.S.C), as well as sub-system, contains its polar opposite. These polar tendencies within each mandala manifest as: male-female, black-white, good-bad, negative-positive, unconscious-conscious, passive-aggressive, love-hate and others. The African Science of the Circle (Mandala) as a symbol of integration and wholeness expresses this path of synthesis between all opposites.

These "Natural Soul Forces" of the mandala are organizing forces of the Innerself (unconscious mind). They lead to concepts, ideas, values and behaviors being organized into some coherent context in conscious behavior. This process of organizing concepts into the context of meaningful conscious patterns of behavior could be referred to as "contextualization". This process allows the participant to undergo the "mystic transformation" from instinctual human to divine human. This process of contextualization of the Soul Forces constitutes the "African Science". The African Science is the accumulated knowledge in the collective consciousness of

3

Africentric people of how to live in tune with the non-human world of Mother nature and the invisible spiritual world of God. This African Science comprises the Heart of Soul.

The Soul Forces or Orisha collectively constitute the Dark Feminine principle or "Mother Nature" forces. They are the different aspects of the natural and non-human world which constitute the unconscious, historical and social mind both at the personal and the collective level. Each Orisha is but another interpretation or representation of the one great Reality—the indwelling Beloved Community.

The Western world, even though unwittingly participating in these Soul Forces, has denied their existence. The Heart of Soul has been repressed as evil, instinctual, chaotic and negative primarily because of its dark and feminine origins in Mother Africa. The "Soul Forces" got repressed in western Freudian psychology under the mask of the "Id".

The scientific world as well as the rest of the world awaits the re-integration of this vital aspect of psychic life. This re-integration of the Soul is necessary in order to restore equilibrium and balance to the rational mind. The birth of that which is highest in humanity always comes from a "return". At this point in history, the "return" would have to constitute an acknowledgement of the Primal Paradise—The Origins—Mother Source—The Mother Root—The Beginnings—Mother Africa Within—the Heart of Soul.

The Call From The Heart Of Soul

The Black consciousness revolution of the Sixties was one manifestation of this call to Center and Return To The Source. There have been other calls to Center throughout the four hundred years of African exile and enslavement in America such as the Marcus Garvey movement and other Pan-African movements. This call to Center was, and is, the spiritual-intuitive consciousness of the right-brain attempting re-integration and establishment of harmony and balance with the rational-logical, scientific worldview. The rational-logical, scientific worldview has been holding, and continues to hold, the Soul and its intuitive-spiritual functions forcibly under repression.

Concomitant with the revolution in Black consciousness during the Civil Rights movement, a revolution in consciousness in many other areas of society, including the scientific field, was underway which would allow for, if not force, the re-integration of the Soul. The dominant sway of the left hemisphere orientation of the brain which once dominated human consciousness gave way to a wave of research and publications. This wave of research produced the split-brain theory, bi-modal consciousness, right-brain consciousness, intuitive-spiritual consciousness and more. One of the foremost thinkers and researchers in this area, Roger Sperry, received a Nobel Prize in 1981 in Medicine and Physiology for his work in split-brain research and, according to Omni Magazine, August, 1983, "has dedicated much of his time now to battling the materialist legacy of Twentieth Century Science".

The central and key issue to the repression of the Soul and its intuitive forces was very much related to ethnicity, I-dentity, economics and power. In order to enslave a people for economic gain, it was first necessary to break their worldview and their connection to their Mother Root, their Heart of Soul. This de-stabilization and de-empowerment process took place, and continues to take place by a programmatic, scientific and systematic assault on the central or core I-dentity structure and ethnic-cultural belief system of those to be repressed and enslaved.

FOR NOTES
Insights, Reflections, Self-Observations

CHAPTER 2:

Ethnicity, Self-image And I-dentity

All cultures evolve a coherent set of images, symbols and values which form the communicational patterns of that culture. These communicational and interactional patterns serve as that culture's Heart of Soul. These communicational patterns operate at both the verbal and the non-verbal levels. Most attitudes, behavioral traits and value references are usually formulated largely at the pre-verbal, unconscious level. The unconscious mind-Soul both programs and is programmed during the growth, maturational and acculturation process through the interactions that the self has within the context of the culture. This programming of the self is designed to guide the individual into certain "tracks" of thinking, perceiving, relating and behaving. The two major track programs of the self which will be discussed in this book are:

1. The "Life-Track" which refers to the cultural themes inherited at birth from the collective ancestral Soul which defines one's mission and purpose for being in this life.
2. The "life-style" which refers to the birth-order and temperamental orientation for interacting in the world and carrying out one's mission.

This "track" and "style" programming is accomplished through establishing symbolic cognitive "screens" of reality. Cognitive screens are screens through which we view the world and come to know reality. Some of these cognitive screens are inherited at birth from the collective genetic storage of archetypal patterns and some are established from interactions with the environment after birth—during the process of growth and maturation.

Some cognitive screens have positively charged symbolic associations and others have negatively charged symbolic associations. The construction of these screens has been done down through history both at the conscious and unconscious levels. The construction of cognitive screens continues to be done today by selectively employing various images, words, symbols, role models to assign certain values of good-bad, positive-negative and desirability-undesirability to one worldview as opposed to another. The individual learns from and internalizes the cognitive screens that he or she comes into contact with within the representational context of his/her cultural values and beliefs. This involves a process of (1.) "influence", a transferal of symbol-psychic energy between the various screens, (2.) a process of internalization and incorporation (taking-in of the various screens and their associated symbols and values), (3.) a process of I-dentification (becoming one with the screens and their associated symbols and values).

The continuity and integrity of the Life-Track (cultural sense of purpose and mission) and life-styles depend upon the internalization and I-dentification of symbolic screens that reinforce cultural symbols, beliefs, values, behaviors and attitudes. Reinforcement rituals may be more geared to reinforce the spiritual (Life-Track) or the material (life-style) by the selective values placed on symbols and images. True cultural I-dentity can only proceed when there is integral continuity between the Life-track and the life- style.

All of these processes of knowing reality and screens of perception are necessary in shaping the self, the I, the soul-personality-ego-character-SOUL in its various facets, both positive and negative. The most frequently used symbolic screens are those most highly identified with and they form the "core" screens of the self.

The core screens of the self then could be true core screens (the Life-Track screen) or a false core screen (one acquired from a preferred life-style which has no integral relationship to the cultural Life-Track).

Screens of the Self

1. Core I-dentity Screen—sexual I-dentity and orientation, ethnicity and all of the associated characteristics of these two. This includes the Life-Track mission that one is born to carry out at the physical, emotional, mental and spiritual levels.

2. Peripheral I-dentity Screen—the more superficial and material aspects of identity. This would include the life-style orientation and the attitudinal-value-behavioral adjustments that one makes during the course of life.

All of reality has to be interpreted through the cognitive symbolic screens of the core and peripheral self. Both of these screens of self are evolved through the formation of the "I" during its interactions and relationships to reality. In this process of interacting with reality, the self may become I-dentified with various symbolic screens which are either reflective of the true core self or the peripheral self. Through the process of mis-I-dentification, the peripheral self may serve as a "core self" but it would be a false core self. For example, black youth identifying with the gold-ladened look are mis-identifying the peripheral self with the true core cultural Self. Black middle-class professionals who have abandoned the Black community for the image of white middle-class life-styles are identifying with the peripheral self and not the core cultural Self.

Knowing reality through the true core center of the Self empowers the "I" of the individual to grow in Self-control, Self-mastery and Self-transcendence. Knowing reality through the false center of self often leads the growth of the soul-personality-character along many maladaptive, deviant and self-destructive paths. Individuation or the achievement of a well balanced, integrated and empowered state is the outcome of growth and maturation through the true core center of the Self.

I-dentification, identity and one's view of reality are central to the process of formulating a well-integrated self-concept, sense of self and ego. For it is from this well formulated self-concept that we derive our view of the world and are able to intervene in changing and creating our reality. This process of deriving a view of reality is generally referred to as "cognition." Cognition simply means "to know". The process of deriving a view of ourselves—the I—in relationship to reality will be referred to as "I-dentification". Down through the centuries, there have been two major recognized modes of "knowing" reality and formulating a sense of I-dentity. The oldest which is related to the right-brain is known as the intuitive-spiritual-rational-holistic mode. The newest means of knowing reality, which is related to the left-brain is known as the logical-materialistic-rational-lineal mode.

I-dentification, from an Africentric perspective is a continuous process, involving both of these modes, that starts before birth and continues after death. The continuity of this process of I-dentification can be perceived if we imagine the mind-Soul-Self as composed of a series of continuous hierarchically arranged screens (imago-templates) that filter reality. Imago-template screens are conglomerates of M.I.S.E.S.C. It is through these screens that we receive our impressions, make our decisions and judgments and carry out our actions. We interact with the world, both inner spiritual world and outer material world, as a result of our decisions, judgments and actions based on these screens. The outcome and consequence of our interactions with the world based on these inner screens of reality, determine our self-concept, sense of self-esteem and I-dentity. These inner screens are comprised of the various symbols and metaphors that have accumulated down through the many centuries of evolution of the material, animal and human world.

Imago Template Screens

These screens will here-in-after be referred to variously as metaphoric screens, imagoes, imago-templates or imago-symbolic-energy-complex-systems. The latter designation is more truly representative of the complex hooked-together associative nature of these inner screens. All of these titles are used interchangeable because these titles show up in various belief systems, psychological and spiritual literature. The use of the various titles is intended not to confuse but to help the reader make the necessary connections to the various literary materials that may be read.

These imago-template screens transcend cultural, sexual, ethnic, regional and religious differences. These imago screens comprise the major symbols that the soul-personality-ego-character is called upon to interact with during the growth-maturational process within the context of any given cultural, geographical and time context. These imago-template screens are comprised of metaphors, myths, symbols, sentiments, instincts, value judgments and emotive-drives. An imago then is more than a physical image. It is a complex energy field comprising all the elements of sentiment, metaphor, myth, instinct, value judgement and emotive-drive. The Imago-template screen transcends time and reaches into the past and future as if they were the present moment.

Some of the major symbolic imago-template screens would be those of the mother-feminine, female, witch-bitch, the old wise woman, father-masculine, male, the old wise man, child-trickster, joker, savior, hero, shadow and others. These screens are mainly found in groupings or clusters of associations which have been variously referred to throughout psychological and philosophical literature as complexes, imagoes, archetypes and symbols. They have also been referred to as the "gods of the unconscious mind". In African and Eastern tradition, these complex screens have been variously referred to as neters, orisha, gods and soul forces. They are believed to house the invisible world of Spirit or Soul.

Many of these screens are passed on genetically in the hereditary process as engrams and are further unfolded and enhanced during their transit through the developmental-maturational fields of consciousness. In Eurocentric-Western psychological tradition, until very recently, it has always been thought that the enfant was born with a "clean slate" as a mind. In other words, it was assumed that the genetic code was smart enough to determine such minute details as the fingerprints and other physical structures but was not smart enough to determine mental and personality traits. Scientific Western psychology is now changing and abandoning its clean-slate beliefs and adopting a "written-on-slate" belief about the natal mind.

The child is now believed to be born with a host of memory and information screens which later determine temperamental and cognitive styles. The archetypal psychology of Carl Jung contributed much information in this area. These screens not only apply to individual growth and maturation but also to the growth and maturation of groups and cultures. A common collective cultural screen would be called it's "worldview", "representational system", "umwelt", "ancestral mind", "group soul", "Zamani", "Life-Track" and others. A representational worldview is the Life-track of dominant themes, metaphors, coping skills, survival mechanisms, inventions, worship systems and philosophical beliefs that guide the growth and interactions of a group of people.

Collectively these metaphorical screens of the innerself, belong to the Great Black Mother—The Soul—Mother Africa Within, the Base and Mother Root of the human evolutionary tree. The Soul is the representational system from which all human culture, cognition and perception evolves. The Soul as Heart and Center of cognition is the worldview of people of African decent, whether this descent is recognized or unrecognized, whether owned or unowned.

What Is The Re-emerging Dark Mother Or Dark Feminine

The metaphor of the Re-Emerging Dark Mother, like any true metaphor, can not be defined in exact terms, one could go on for days explaining IT, but the real understanding of IT can only be had from experiencing IT. The experience of IT would best be described through those moments and processes that most closely puts us in touch with the transcendental-spiritual aspects of the self-personality-ego-character-SOUL. Some of those moments come during such experiences as altered states of consciousness experienced in such phenomena as "getting the spirit", "getting happy", out of body experiences, trance states, intuitive experiences and precognitive phenomena.

The Re-Emerging Dark Feminine as the Ground Of Being is an ancient wisdom energy system, the ancient wisdom system that allowed Africans to build the pyramids and the Sphinx. It is the type of consciousness that the rational, logical, scientific mind has never been able to decipher, analyze or understand.

The Good Dark Mother   **The Terrible Dark Mother**

Some aspects of the Re-Emerging Dark Mother as metaphor can be apprehended through the names and descriptions applied to Her down through the centuries. Some names, titles and descriptions of the Dark Mother and Her associated White counterparts in Her positive and negative aspects include: Isis, Hathor, Mut, Nut, Ma-at, Bast, Bastet, Kali, Shakti, Sophia (Gnostics)—Wisdom (Greeks) symbolized as the dove, Erishkegal/Inanna (Sumerian), Yemanya, Oshun, Erzulie, Oya (Goddess of the Cemetaries), Inhasa (Goddess of the Winds and Hurricanes), Mary, Mary Magdeline, The Old Wise Woman, Lilith (Adam's first Wife—Fate), The Bride of God, Prima Materia (alchemist), Gaia, The Holy Spirit, The Divine Feminine, The Divine Harlot, The Hag, The Witch, The Bitch, The Whore, The Wench, The Slut, The Troll, The Eternal Feminine, The Mother of God, The Mother of the Philosophers, Shekinah, Lady of the Perfect Black, The Night Mother, The Guardian of the Law, Savior Goddess, The Great Mother, Athena, Aphrodite, Astarte, Chokma (ancient Hebrew), The Triple Goddess (life, death, rebirth), Three Eves, Artemis (creatrix), Selene (preserver), Hecate (crone, destroyer), Demeter and Persephone, Cybele, Subterranean Queen of Heaven, Patroness of Freedom and Nature, The Black Cloud, The New Jerusalem and The Shadow.

The Re-Emerging Dark Mother can be known also through her manifestations. She has been worshipped down through history as the Earth Mother in such forms as underground springs and wells; as black meteorite stones including the Holy Kaaba Stone at Mecca. She has been and continues to be worshiped in her manifestations as rivers, oceans and wind.

The Re-Emerging Dark Mother is the Goddess of transformations, maturation, and death-rebirth. She is the guardian of change, aging, deterioration, decay and death. She demands that we confront the death of soul-personality-ego-character-SOUL.

The Re-Emerging Dark Feminine is The Coming Science Of The Soul—The Science of the inner "Light", the Coming Forth By Day. All past memories belong to the realm of the Dark Feminine, the past which fades into darkness, the beginnings which are shrouded in darkness. The Emerging Dark Feminine represents the return of the deepest and therefore highest forces of the Soul—as symbolized in the Beloved Community.

The African Science is a Science of Wholeness. As such, one of its oldest symbols is the Sacred Circle, or 360 degrees of knowledge, pictured in one of its ancient forms as the Great Serpent that swallows its tail (the Uroborous). The Uroborous, as primal mandala thus symbolizes the self-fecundating and self-regenerative powers inherent in the Soul of humanity, the Soul of Nature and the Cosmos.

The African Science of the Soul therefore differs radically and essentially in its focus and intended outcome from the European science of psychology. The western or European science is primarily focused on a rational-logical documentation of external and material reality as extensions and projections of the ego. Western science's primary approach is one of curing symptoms which are seen as the material, visible manifestations of disease. On the contrary, the traditional African Science has always been, is now, and forever shall be, focused on the invisible forces of the innerself—the Soul. It's emphasis, as such, is one of healing the underlying psychic causes of disharmony between the body and the Soul. Further it is a science of growth, health, harmony and wholeness between the non-visible world of "Spirit" and the visible material world. Both are seen as equally alive, vital and necessary to the growth and developmental processes.

FOR NOTES
Insights, Reflections, Self-Observations

CHAPTER 3:
The Repression Of The Heart

The Repression Of The Screen Of The Positive Shadow

This ancient Soul-Centered worldview of the Dark Feminine celebrated worldwide in the pre-Christian era of human development, was eclipsed with the rise of European-western, rational-logical, materialistic, left-brain psychology and religion. This ancient system of self-unfoldment, maturation, human-spiritual deification was systematically and scientifically smashed and put into repression—but not destroyed.

The repression of the Dark Feminine has lasted down through the centuries because of the continued repressive forces of the mainstream rational-logical-masculine "white superiority screen". This imago-screen of White superiority/Black inferiority has been perpetuated by all the systems comprising the mainstream, masculine-oriented, Europcentric culture which has dominated the world for the past two or more thousand years. The intuitive-feminine, Soul-centered worldview has essentially not been reintegrated into the consciousness of modern humanity. This lack of integration of the feminine, Soul-centered worldview leaves modern-scientific man, and woman, in a state known as the "dark night of the soul". As Carl Jung implied in his book, Modern Man In Search Of His Soul, if we do not find It (the Soul) soon, it may be too late.

Divided And Dual Reality Screens Of Un-Knowing Reality

Even through African-Americans and African-Carribeans were separated from their homeland and the culture of Soul was put into repression, they were never separated from their Souls. Africans in the diaspora are very much still guided today in their attitudes, values and behaviors by this underlying worldview of Soul.

The Kerner Commission Report and the Coleman Report coming out of the turbulence of the Sixties, documented that the American society and character exists as two separate, unequal societies and character structures. One of these societies constitutes Eurocentric-white-mainstream America. The other society constitutes Africentric-Black, non-mainstream America. Those individuals who are not included in the mainstream culture with its exclusive Eurocentric focus, are hampered by social, emotional, environmental, economic and family factors which impede or totally block their cognitive ("knowing") process. The exclusive Eurocentric focus of mainstream American culture does not recognize any cultural reality outside of its own as valid of representation. This results in a process of mis-education and mis-knowing which has far reaching ramifications for the individual and the collective of both White and Black societies.

Those individuals not included in the mainstream culture are hampered in their full cognitive development in both the left-brain, rational-logical, scientific-materialistic mode and the apperceptual-intuitive mode of the right-brain. In the society in which non-mainstream individuals find themselves, too often the stress is on acquiring academic knowledge in order to obtain and defend material gains. This over-emphasis on developing the left-brain, materialist approach to life supercedes the development of the cognitive mode central to Black cultural development—namely the intuitive, Soul-Centered cognitive mode. This creates an unknowing dynamic that has far reaching implications for the developing self-concepts of the African-American individual and the cultural group. It is to this dynamic of knowing-unknowing of the cultural self that Carter G. Woodson addressed himself when he wrote his book, the Miseducation Of the Negro.

Frequently Blacks have withdrawn themselves from the oppressive and repressive representational system of White society but have not defined and enhanced the representational system of the Cultural Self that would empower Black I-dentity. They have, like the White culture, frequently refused to explore the intuitive-spiritual modes of Africentric culture. Knowing and Un-knowing relates, at the bottom line, to cultural relevancy and cultural irrelevancy; to cultural survival or cultural annihilation.

Because of the European educational and acculturational process that African-Americans are processed through, the right brain intuitive-spiritual process is almost as inaccessible to them as it formerly was to Whites. In the absence of a cultural frame of reference through which we define and name ourselves in the I-dentity and developmental processes, we find ourselves often employing other's terms for us and our behavior which ultimately leads to a mis-naming and mis-labelling process.

The mis-naming, mis-labelling and mis-usage of words that are used to help formulate Black-Child development, self-concept and I-dentity formation, have contributed greatly to mis-channelling of innate spiritual energies. This mis-naming process has lead to a dissipation of drive and motivation to become mature, independent and Self-Realized beings. We are turned away from, and against, that which is naturally us by the present Eurocentric representation of reality in which we find ourselves. This brings about an unknowing process not only on behalf of Blacks but also on behalf of Whites. The Mother Root foundation of human evolution as the imago-template of Blackness is not available for integration into consciousness as a positive by either group.

The intuitive-spiritual, soul-centered mode of cognition which is central to, and is the heart of, the imago-template of Blackness is therefore suppressed daily in western culture. This imago-template is not only central to the maturation and individuation of Black people but to all people. This suppression takes place through every system of society dealing with the socialization and acculturation of the soul-personality-ego-character. Psychology, religion, the educational experience and, even more so, mass-media, public images and symbols play important roles in the unknowing process. The materialistic-individualist, logical, perceptual, self-centered symbols and life-styles get embedded in the minds of the young through subliminal images and symbols, with intent and outcome of affecting them from the cradle of the grave. The internalization of these images, which are often destructive of human and natural life, lead to the awakening of the archetypal patterns of CHAOS.

The over-valuation of this materialistic mode of representing the Self as positive and valid is done to the exclusion of the African-Eastern, intuitive-spiritual-rational representational mode. It is the intuitive cognitive mode which is the original, indigenous cultural mode of all people but especially of people of direct and claimed African descent. The intuitive cognitive mode of knowing reality and the self is more right-brain oriented which relies upon the creative channels of the mind (right-brain) called the Soul. The center of this right-brain cognitive mode, as taught by the ancient Egyptians, is the heart rather that the head.

Mandala Diagram

FOR NOTES
Insights, Reflections, Self-Observations

CHAPTER 4:

The Repression and Suppression of the Soul

Socio-Cultural Consequences of the Lack of Integration of the Soul

Many years of working in the major psychiatric clinics and a variety of community centers, have led me to conclude that many of the theoretical constructs developed to analyze behavior and treat behavioral disturbances in mainstream Western culture are inadequate when applied to non-mainstream cultural groups. The inadequacy of theoretical constructs lies in the fact of their having completely omitted the important ethnic and cultural factor of Soul. These psychological theories therefore, do not apply, and can not be applied, cross-culturally to non-mainstream cultural groups without adequate modification and revision.

The families within the American mainstream culture are defined and directed in their developmental processes by a representational system of formal and informal networks designed to support and enhance their identity, existence and survival. By and large, these supportive formal networks consist of the decision-making and policy-setting bodies in the areas of politics, economics, sociology, psychology, medicine, philosophy, religion and a host of informal networks and supportive structures.

The mainstream "representational system", however, is not constructed to represent and support families "outside of the mainstream", outside of the "system", outside of the "white superiority screen" in the same manner during their developmental process. The necessary Black healthy representation and support do not happen to any planned, organized extent in psychology, education, religion or any of the other areas that impact, influence and mould the development of a healthy self-concept and wholesome sense of I-dentity in Black people. Often to the contrary, the "representational system" which supports the formal networks of the American mainstream culture, in many respects, is designed to exclude a positive self image of the families who find themselves outside of this mainstream culture. The "white superiority screen" is designed to induce in people of color the feeling of inferiority, negativity and low esteem of self, family and culture.

If one could isolate out the X-factor, the basic ingredient, which regulates the influence and the impact of formal and informal systems upon growth, development and functional family structure, one would ultimately isolate out the factor of a coherent system of ideas, symbols and images related to that culture's ancestral past, core-mythology and worldview. It is through this coherent cultural symbolic system that the cultural heritage can be employed to bind or "yoke" the I-dentity of the individual, family and community as a unit. It is this "yoking" or "binding" system which houses the moral, ethical and spiritual precepts of a culture and which determine that culture's higher mental-spiritual functions of bonding, sharing, unity, will, motivation, judgement, insight, synthesis, integration, transcendence, transformation and creativity.

It is to this coherent and determinative system of ideas, behaviors and creative functions that we apply the name "group soul" or "representational system", and herein-after will be referred to alternatively as the "Life-Track". This later designation is opposed to the designation of "Life-style Issues and Themes" which refer more to the material, behavioral/emotional interactions related to birth-order, parental preference, and concrete manifested behavior as taught in Adlerian psychology.

Traditionally, Africentric people have always presumed and paid the highest respect to this central "Life-Track" of determinative ideas, behaviors, symbols and creative expressions. They viewed this realm not as an isolated, or even individualistic function of development and I-dentity, but as an expression of the higher invincible natural-Soul Forces, the archetypal collective intelligent mind.

This collective mind was felt to be manifesting through the "unbroken circle" which includes individual, family, community, society, nation, world and cosmos. In the absence of this collective cultural worldview we find ourselves estranged, lonely and often lost in foreign mazes of the mind and realms of self negation.

The Oppressive Shadow Of Harlem

Sisters sitting on stoops
bellies sagging, sad looks saying
save us from this sinking sunk-hole
situated in the center of saturated dreams,
leading to dimmer realms of despair and darkness.

Bubblegum blowing mamas
and lollipop licking grandmas
look out upon a reality
rancid with deception, neglect and gore
grasping at the last glimmers of a fading feminine
whose absence means a lost of soul.

Babies beaming with bright innocence
unsuspecting of the blight
built into their already bungled existence
Bantered back and forth
by a beleaguered society
and bombed-out parents
battling for better buys
of bagged poison.
Unaware of the fading, fastly receding glimmer
in the eyes of the children.

> *Eyes that become blank*
> *and unblinking*
> *as they butt-up against the bland reality*
> *of their bondage.*

The Eclipse

The holistic Africentric, Soul-Centered view of reality and cognition was shattered with the cognitive switch from right-brain, heart-centered knowing. This switch came with the Europeanization of African culture and consciousness and the subsequent dispersion of Africans from their homeland. This traditional Africentric holistic worldview underwent systematic and scientific attempts to destroy and/or repress it. A part of the repression of this holistic mode of cognition was the labels, negative associations and values placed upon it, such as: "primitive", "evil", "negative", "sinister", "feminine", and "Gauche". These terms, in a white male-oriented culture, take on connotative associations of negativity, were assigned to, and associated with Blacks and Blackness.

Thus a worldview, a whole mode of cognition became submerged and relegated to negativity and oblivion. However, because of its rootedness in what "Is", the Soul-Centered worldview survived this onslaught and continued to flourish, under both repression and oppression in various creative ways through other religious guises, artistic and social forms. It rarely, however, was allowed overt expression and representation in its own right within the context of the oppressive cultures in which it became entrapped.

This African cognitive style was masked over by a representational system (Euro-centric worldview) with a cognitive style which frequently has just the polar opposite set of values; just the polar opposite of ethical, aesthetic and creative considerations. This alien representational system constituted the European left-brained mode of logical, exploitative—materialism. This rational-logical, "scientific", materialistic, individualistic approach to reality has until very recently, been perpetuated and represented as the only true, valid and civilized mode of cognition. It was no doubt a necessary developmental stage in the evolution of the human psychic structure.

Its disadvantages and limitations, however, lie in its approach to developmental issues such as birth, separation, parenting, maturation, death, transcendence and deification. All of which are necessarily colored by its materialistic approach to reality.

Those engaged solely in this view of reality find it difficult, if not impossible to make the leap from the belief in material causality to spiritual causality. This western, materialistic approach to the Divine Creative-Force-Within can only at best, be intellectualized and rationalized. God and religion remain outside to be studied as dogma, the rewards of which must await a final Judgement Day after death. In this worldview, the ego instead of the Soul remains the central organizing principle of reality. As a result of this dislocation from, and lack of proper integration of, the primal worldview of Soul with its non-material, spiritual forces, the Western World finds itself in a ecological, spiritual, moral imbalance which is taking its toll at all levels of existence—the psychological, social, religious, scientific, ecological, and geological. The lack of integration of the Black Goddess-the SOUL in its positive aspect as COMMUNITY, causes a reverse awakening of the negative aspect of the Goddess as the archetype of CHAOS.

The Casting Of The Shadow

Regardless of culture or ethnic group, individuals nor families exist in isolation; rather they are embedded in and impacted by, formal and informal networks and systems that comprise their Collective Souls, Group Souls or "representational systems". These representational systems consist of symbols, values, beliefs and practices that have significance for the overall adaptation and empowerment of the individual and group. They relate through time and space to the deeper underlying structures of human consciousness—the invisible, spiritual Soul Forces. Obviously some cultures are more related to these underlying structures of evolutionary consciousness than others.

At times, these Group Souls or "representational systems" are supportive of growth and maturation and bring about cohesion; at other times they are disruptive and destructive of family and individual unity and the growth/maturational process. Various ethnic groups interpret and assign relative values to their various "representational systems" of human behavior and culture. Pierre Janet, a French psychiatrist, who was one of Freud's colleagues and teachers, referred to this process of assignment of values of preferred worth to superficial and relative structures in society, as "competitive value setting".

During this process, one group creates the illusion that its culture and "representational system" is more legitimate, advanced, civilized, and of more value than another. Those values and images not included in the mainstream "representational system" are suppressed, repressed and reduced to a negative status. Those people who find their cultural values and heritage excluded and repressed as negative have two alternatives, (1) they are ultimately forced to identify with, and are reduced to, a projected negative image of inferiority from the dominant culture as its shadow, (2) they continuously fight and struggle to represent their cultural worldview as a living, dynamic positive.

This "negative", rejected and projected shadowy image of mainstream culture, especially of its Black aspect, continues to be perpetuated today through various systems comprised within the major Euro-American representational network, i.e., education, science, politics, religion, psychology, economics, and so forth. This is complicated further by the added favor of the electronics media which reinforces and magnifies the projected cultural values of "White is right" and "Black is wrong". This projected, un-integrated content in the American psychic structure has set up a duality which comprises warring factions that threatens to rend it asunder unless harmonized.

This devaluation of the archetype of Blackness and the African-American representational worldview is at the gross level symbolized by the exclusive focus of the current mainstream-European representational system on the logical-material-sequential aspect of reality. This negative valuation of Blackness occurs not only by the dominant society, but frequently by African-Americans themselves, thereby dragging many other aspects of their collective cultural "representational system" into the lacuna or "empty space" of the negative shadowy aspect of the unconscious mind.

FOR NOTES
Insights, Reflections, Self-Observations

CHAPTER 5:

The Ethnic Screening Template as the Determinant of Socio-cultural Interactions

The Ethnic Screening Template as an invented imago-template of the innerself is the primary determinant of the individual and collective representational system in Ameri-Eurocentric mainstream culture as it interacts and relates to non-European, non-mainstream cultures. This is elaborated in Earl Conrad's book—The Invention of the Negro. It is this imago-template which is primarily responsible for the devaluation of Blackness and the obscuration of the Dark Feminine. This image-template screen is continuously nurtured and kept alive through its umbilical connections with the constitutional representational system that govern American and Eurocentric, mainstream cultures and reality.

The images and symbols that are created and perpetuated through the institutions of the American culture, as they are filtered through the Ethnic Screening Template, have a decided preference for white as right—good and black as wrong—evil. The other template of the self-the Soul, the heart of the true individuated Self, stands in dynamic opposition to, and is the reverse aspect of the reality of the Ethnic Screening Template of Self. "The Self as Soul-Centered" constitutes the true template of Self of all human beings. It is the template of the individuated, perfected, spiritualized Self which is indwelling. It is represented as the full development of the soul-personality-ego-character-SOUL—the LIGHT, as reflected in Jesus the Christ, Horus, Hathor, Ra, Isis—as models of the fully Self-Realized Being—The Divine Being—The Beloved Community.

The switch from self-responsibility for this inner process of Soul-Development, Self-Transcendence and Union with the higher spiritualizing levels of consciousness came with the switch from right-brain, intuitive development to left-brain, logical-material development. This switch takes the mystique and responsibility of communicating with the inner spiritual world of God away from the individual and projects it outside-into the sky. This eclipse or switch places the responsibility for communicating with this spiritual realm in the hands of a few intermediaries who would be the priests, preachers, ministers as spiritual power-brokers. The Ethnic Screening Template as the false dominant template of Self operates predominantly from the rational, material-centered, masculine-oriented, left-brain whereas the original-True Template of Self operates predominantly from the intuitive, spiritual-centered right-brain and heart as center of the Soul. These templates affect the person through the life-cycle and beyond the grave in their representation of self/not-self, desirability/ undesirability, lovability/unlovability, self-worth, self-esteem, self-concept and I-dentity/non-I-dentity.

The Internalization Of The Ethnic Screening Template

Racial representation and differentiation begins as early as two-and-a-half to three years of age for persons living in racist societies. Some psychologists believe that racial differentiation and preference begins as early as in-utero. An example of this early differentiation of racial preference would be a 2 y.o. Black female who was entertained in my waiting room with a mixed pile of dolls representing a Black family and a White family. She spontaneously sorted through the pile and selected only the white dolls for her play while pushing all of the black dolls aside.

From this early pre-verbal stage of ethnic-racial differentiation onward, depending upon the external and internal feedback that the child receives in helping her to structure reality in relationship to the Total Self, ethnic-racial representation undergoes:

a. a developmental progression towards resolution and wholeness or,

b. a developmental retrogression, lack of closure and resolution which ends in stasis and foreclosure of the growth of the soul-personality-ego-character-SOUL. This is well documented by the research findings reported in the book by Stuart Hauser, Black and White Identity Formation.

It is also at this early, pre-verbal level of racial-ethnic differentiation that the images, words, symbols of the invisible template of self become operant in structuring the attitudes and cognitive style that is largely passed on through unconscious, non-verbal cultural interactional patterns and child-rearing practices.

The Ethnic Screening Template, the false template of self, also structures mainstream institutional practices, such as education, religion, housing, social welfare and health systems to perpetuate its evil intent. All of these systems serve to reinforce the differential value between Black and White at the group mind-Soul level.

The major ethnic differentiation imago templates affecting African-American and European-American relations at the individual and group levels are further designated into the internalized imagoes of Black male (BM), Black female (BF), White male (WM), White female (WF). This cluster of four imagoes or schema make up a sub-template in the pre-conscious mind which is central in the representational system of the majority, if not all individuals exposed to Eurocentric culture, values and beliefs. (Schema are internal patterns of organizing, perceiving and acting on reality, whether outer or inner).

Whites handle these inner imagoes, especially those of blackness, differently from the majority of Blacks. Most frequently, Blacks handle the inner imagoes of whiteness in a distorted manner similar to how Whites embody these imagoes, and therefore, come across as an imitation of whiteness with its consequent "affectations" of superiority. We are all familiar with the expression applied to certain Blacks of island descent colonized by the British, as being "more British than the British".

Each of these imagoes of the Ethnic Screening Template (White male, Black female, etc.), carries its own unique mythology, word symbolism, associations, emotions, sentiments, and behavioral patterns. It is through these major or primary imagoes (templates and sub-templates) that secondary images are interpreted; attitudes are formulated; emotions, sentiments and behaviors are expressed.

Words at some level are synonymous with images. Images differ from imagoes in that images are more external symbolic representations of reality while imagoes are more internally-complexed representations of reality. Imagoes involve values, action systems and triggers to set those associative thought and action patterns into process.

Words and names are employed to create images and illusions by those who wish to oppress and control the minds of others. There is an association of words/images that are employed depending on which of the four schema of the ethnic screening template is in ascendancy (has predominant influence). Each viewed, alone, without the proper context of the others, is an illusion. When all are developed equally, one transcends the inner fragmentary process that the false images/imagoes perpetuate.

The Ethnic Screening Template And The Negative Shadow

This lack of positive and true integration of the Soul into an Euro-American pluralistic representational model as a positive aspect of human consciousness has created an unhealthy and dangerous one-sidedness in Euro-American culture and western civilization in general. This one-sided approach to culture and western civilization continues to generate the illusion of inferiority of people of color and negativity for the color of blackness in all of its associations. The wholeness of the human image has been falsely polarized into two imago screens of reality—the good white screen and the bad black screen. These two screens make up the Ethnic Screening Template—

one White and positive and the other Black and negative—one acceptable as a template of human development and the other rejected and projected as unacceptable as a template of human development.

The degradation, negation and projection outward of the rejected shadowy contents attached to Black images from the White unconscious mind in the illusion of the "Negro", "Nigger", "three-fifth Human" has often resulted in the Black population taking them in and believing them. As a result, there is a subsequent projection of these images among Blacks—outward onto the environment and each other, thus creating a state of obsession and near possession, herein referred to as the Negative-Self Concept Syndrome. This condition has already wrecked havoc and continues to destroy the Black Community with Black-on-Black crime rates reaching phenominally high proportions in statistics such as 84% of crimes against Blacks are committed by Blacks. The death rate from Black males killing Black males in 1976 alone was reported as being higher than the death rate of Black males killed in battle during the whole 10 years of the Vietnam War. These increasing patterns towards violence and aggression also threatens to inundate the larger society.

The goal of development for all individuals, Black as well as White, is to embody (live) a harmonious balance of these imagoes as positive without ignoring their negatives—to create a whole person(ality). In the absence of this inner integration and balancing of imagoes, when one imago is overly developed as positive and as the only valid image of "(Being)" and another is overly developed as negative and is projected outward as ("Sub-Being"), an inner dichotomy develops that leaves a gaping hole, "an empty space" in the mind/Soul. This gaping hole allows the ego to become obsessed/possessed by the energies of the rejected unconscious mind and negative "shadow".

The dissociation of the outer masculine from the inner state of wholeness and integrity of the soul-personality-ego-character results in the inner production of a Black unaccepted and negative self and a White accepted and positive self. This positive-negative separation of the inner feminine occurs in dissociative states of not only White females and males, but in Black females and males. This can be witnessed in such accounts as the books Sybil and The Three Faces

Of Eve. These inner dissociative states of black-evil/white-good could threaten to rend asunder the ego structure of the individual as well as the collective (community, nation.)

Characteristics Of The The Ethnic Screening Imago-template

This imago-template screen is comprised of two interrelated and co-dependent imago-complexes. They are the White Racist Superiority Complex (WRSC)/Black Negative Inferiority Complex (BNIC).

- This combined grouping of opposite imago-symbolic energies is an autonomous complex. This means that it has a mind of its own. It comes and goes according to triggering stimuli and situations which may be associations triggered by colors, sounds, smells, location, position, cyclic change of seasons and holidays.
- This imago-symbolic complex is largely passed on through unconscious, non-verbal modes of childrearing practices and cultural institutions which impact these practices.
- These Soul-Forces are passed on largely through affect and its associations. This constitutes the bonding phenomenon, whereby "affect" units or vibes are passed through verbal and non-verbal modes between bonder-bondee (mother-child, hero-hero worshiper, lover-lover, etc.)
- Religion, education, housing, welfare, health systems all reinforce the differential symbolic value and sense of self-worth/non-worth between Black and White.
- This imago-symbolic screen, template or complex forever desires to increase its power in the soul-personality-ego-character-SOUL structure of the individual-group. The WRSCS/BNSC is designed and programed to be an automatic self-reproducing, self-enhancement system. This system always seeks more power in order to

maintain the necessary illusion of superiority that yields power and demands submission.

- This complex of WRSC/BNIC has a direct relationship of power and growth in the Innerself. The more power taken and surrendered unto the WRSCS, the more powerful the BNIC becomes. The Black Positive Self Concept (BPSC) is, of course, in inverse proportion to the growth an empowerment of the BNIC/WRSC. The more power surrender to the BNIC, the less power remains for the BPSC. The more power gained by the BPSC, the less remains in the BNIC.

- This complex of WRSC/BNIC filters and screens reality both from the outer visible material world and from the inner invisible spiritual world. It flavors both outer reality and inner reality with the differential values of white-good, black-bad; material-positive, spiritual-negative; masculine-superior, feminine-inferior; logical, intellectual, outer God-Positive; spiritual, intuitive, inner God-Negative. All systems of society reinforce these differential values of White as good, Black as bad by the type of service rendered, the type of diagnosis given, the type of housing and neighborhood assignment, the approach to education and the type of curriculum design, the type of images employed in the church to symbolize God and the devil.

- At the individual attitudinal-value-behavioral level, this imago-symbolic complex is situated between the outer self (ego) and the inner Self (unconscious, paraconscious, subconscious, Soul). It is mostly housed in the zone just before conscious awareness (preconscious).

- At the group-collective level, this imago-symbolic complex is situated between the two societies (White/Black) and constitutes the "veil", the "Pall" (W.E.B. DuBois), the "wall" (M.L. King, Jr.). This wall, from the Black side, is translucent and elastic, yet impenetrable. It allows Blacks to interpenetrate and "see", yet not fully participate in all facets and aspects of White life.

From the White side, the wall is relatively opaque and non-flexible and does not allow Whites to interpenetrate nor "see", and only minimally participate in the various facets of Black life.

- Allegorically, Ralph Ellison, in his book "Invisible Man", gives a living description of the "Wall", "Veil", "The Ethnic Screening Template".

- The Ethnic Screening imago-symbolic complex is nurtured and kept alive through its umbilical connections with the larger societal representational system (the constitution and government) and the images and symbols that are perpetrated through its institutions. The 3/5 human being designation of African-Americans in the preamble of the constitution serves as the template for African-American definition. This definition serves as the representation and symbolization in and through the various systems of society representing and extending this constitutional doctrine into everyday American Bi-cultural reality.

- The Ethnic Screening imago-symbolic complex casts a negative shadow upon, and covers up reality for, both Black and White alike. The issue of Blackness and Femininity are the most repressed and guilt ridden issues of the Euro-American society and of European culture in general. This fear of the Black Feminine allows the Black woman greater access into the white mainstream even today than the Black male. There remains a fear, hatred, envy and fascination for the repressed Black Feminine in all of its aspects of, death, earth, mother nature, night, creativity, seasonal changes, bodily cycles and functions.

- The Ethnic Screening Template consists of a complex network of filters or screens that filter and distort reality through the assignment of "competitive values". The competitive values assigned are:

White	Black
right	wrong
good	bad
positive	negative
desirable	undesirable
superior	inferior
day	night
light	darkness
cultural	uncultural
civilized	primitive
strong	weak
valuable	non-valuable
beautiful	ugly
intelligent	illiterate
mannerable	violate
intellectual	physical

Four Major Sub-filters Of The Ethnic Screening Template

(In order of positive affect-valance assigned by the mainstream Euro-centric society)

Positive	Negative
1. WM—White Male	3. BF—Black Female
2. WF—White Female	4. BM—Black Male

Incoming impressions are screened by these filters and their relative values of goodness and badness, thus reinforcing the symbolic values, sentiments and prejudices of these filters.

Each imago carries its own mythology, word-symbol associations, emotions, values, sentiments, attitudes and behaviors. One imago usually has ascendency in the soul-personality-ego-character-SOUL while the others are in the descendent mode.

Superior Mode –ascendent, dominant functions

Inferior Mode –descendent, background functions, "repressed"

Each imago-template is built up of successive layers of schema. These schema have degrees of affect-value-valance. For example, there are different degrees of positivity and negativity assigned.

	high		high
Positive	medium	Negative	medium
	low		low

- These schema and imago-templates exist in groups of opposites and are like muscles—the more they are utilized, the stronger they become. The over-utilization of one may cause the inhibition of the other.
- When one imago-template gains a certain density, it can precipitate an action on the other aspects of soul-personality-ego-character-SOUL at the individual and/or group level.
- All projections into the outer world depend upon these and other internal imago-templates.
- All learning and cognition depend upon these and similar internal schema/imago-templates.
- These internal imago-templates handle the transference of symbolic psycho-spiritual energy.
- They determine transactional mechanisms and interactional patterns.
- These imago-templates are affected and influenced by magnetism which can be induced by hypnotism, meditation, visualization, music and "influence" from others who have a high charge (magnetic charge).
- All of the imago-templates or Soul Forces contribute to, and reinforce one's image of Self and sense of I-dentity to some degree.

- "Negro", "nigger", "Three-fifths Human Being" are all projections from the White culture's collective denial of its African origins.
- Blacks internalize these imagoes of oppression (Nigger, Negro, Three-fifths Human Being), which then become autonomous in their soul-personality-ego-characters-SOULS. Whites reinternalize their collated phantoms from the Nigger, Negro etc—their denied and projected Black I-dentity.
- The WRSC/BNIC is a state of collective obsession bordering on the brink of national psychosis, a possession.
- The internalized images of oppression from this imago-template create inner disunity, fragmentation and move both Blacks and Whites further away from their true centers—their core I-dentity as a collective Community.
- The WRSC/BNIC imago-template sets up a dual reality requiring a dual set of defenses to deal with everyday life, thus the proverbial "Schizophrenic position" of Black Americans.

  The Anti-Self Syndrome, the Anti-Cathectic Self (negatively charged self), so frequently demonstrated in Black behavior.

  In the European-American, the schizophrenic position is characterized as the christian, yet un-spiritual and unnatural, power-lust attitudes and behaviors of Whites.

- White Racist Superiority Complex/Black Negative Inferiority Complex affects the executive functions of will power, judgement, insight, reality-testing, object and essence relations of both White and Blacks.
- These negative internalized images of blackness in both Black and White societies prevent full utilization of the creative energies of the right-brain/the Soul/Innerself.

The "Negro", "Nigger", image prevents the projection of the "true Blackness" schema while providing energy for projection of the negative shadow.

- The symbmolic psycho-spiritual energy associated with "Mother-Africa-Within" (and without)—the True Shadow and imago of Primal Blackness—the Soul—is filtered through the illusion or false image of blackness.

- Without resolution of the negative shadow cast over the Black image (which would mean validation of Blackness as the central symbol of the Soul), the Soul's energies are not only unaccessible for harmonious integration into the conscious mind, but can be dangerous if integration is attempted without transformation. This holds true for not only African-Americans but especially for Europeans of whatever the nationality.

Incoming impressions are screened by the four sub-templates of White male, White female, Black male and Black female. A quantitative and qualitative amount of incoming stimuli are attracted to and filters through whichever imago-template is in ascendancy in the soul-personality-ego-character-SOUL. Each sub-template has a degree of specificity for certain images/stimuli.

Each sub-template is built up of successive layers of schema (ideas, emotions, motives for actions). These schema have positive/negative values that are conditioned by the sub-templates. Environmental and cultural impressions are gathered and screened through these sub-templates as they represent themselves in a symbolic form to the conscious mind as the interpretation of reality. Since schema have a characteristic electro-magnetic valence-charge, they have the ability to somewhat cancel each other or facilitate dominance of either plus or minus charges. The sub-template has its own valence and/or values through which incoming impressions are subsequently screened and symbolized. The sub-template could have a variable valence ranging from highly positive, medium positive, slightly positive, about neutral, slightly negative, moderately negative, strongly negative and so on.

Ascending/Descending (in-remission)

Black Male – BM	(positive ntu units)
Black Female – BF	(positive ntu units)
White Male – WM	(positive ntu units)
White Female – WF	(positive ntu units)
Black Male – BM	(negative ntu units)
Black Female – BF	(negative ntu units)
White Male – WM	(negative ntu units)
White Female – WF	(negative ntu units)

Complete Opposites

B.M.	(+)	W.F.	(-)
B.F.	(+)	W.M.	(-)
B.M.	(-)	W.F.	(+)
B.F.	(-)	W.F.	(+)

(ntu units are soul force units and will be explained in a later chapter)

Negative core self-image ntu units in descendence (suppression, repression) require more total expenditure of vital force on behalf of the individual to keep them in the inferior mode of suppression. Whereas, negative (non-core) or peripheral self-image ntu units in descendence or in the inferior mode do not require an unusual or abnormally taxing amount of Vital Force to keep them in suppression because these (non-core) self-image units are not as highly charged as the core-self-image units. The non-core self ntu-image units exist as peripheral, superficial identity elements or fragmented, segmented, separated images of the whole.

Positive self-image ntu units in descendence (suppression, repression) require more total expenditure of Vital Force on behalf of the ego to keep them in the inferior mode of suppression, and repression because they are core-I-dentity elements. The concept of "primary repression" in non-mainstream cultures therefore takes on added dimensions beyond repression of the negative instincts of the Ground. The primary repression involves a repression of the Core-Cultural Self as Black and Spiritual. To the extent that racists have cast the Black image negatively and to the extent that Blacks have accepted it, they are actually left to identify with the only image projected to them as a positive image, the White image.

To the extent that Blacks adopt this image as their self-image, is to the extent that they define and reinforce their own self-hate and self-negation. In the eyes of the White man, it is viewed as the extent to which the Black man "wants to be like Whites". The implications, of course, being that Blacks feel so negative about themselves that they have to reject themselves. This further supports the negative self-concept theory of Blacks and The White Racist Superiority Concepts of Whites.

Self Perpetuating Dynamics Of The Ethnic Screening Template

The schema and sub-templates of the Ethnic Screening Template are flexible, impressionable and allow new elements to be incorporated, depending on the experience and quality of incoming impressions. When an impression is encountered which does not have a schema or sub-template, it first impinges at the interphase level, creates a schema of an associated symbolic order to the character of the impinging stimulus category. This created schema is altered in a layering manner, depending upon subsequent experience. The schema, image and ultimately the sub-template can be altered or layered and manipulated by fantasy and imagination (visualization) as well as perception from external reality, but most importantly by the execution of will (choice, decision, action and change).

The final conscious image-symbol of Self is composed of various combinations of the four imagoes with relative combination and fusion of the different imagoes. Since the various branches of science have proven that humankind has a common African origin—basically everyone has at the root of their consciousness, the Black Image-Mother Africa Within (The Dark Feminine), against and through, which they filter, compare and juggle their various images and self conceptualizations.

All projections depend upon these inner imago-schema, as Schilder states:

"It is to the existence of these 'schemata' that we owe the power of projection, or recognition of posture, movement, and locality beyond the limits of our own bodies to the end of some instrument held in the hand".

Therefore, it is logical to assume that the projection of race follows these same principles.

Imago-Template Transformation Exercises

Exercise A-1   Conscientizing and transforming names, word images and visual images which perpetuate the unclean spirit, the negative shadow, the racist-ethnic screening template.

1. Have student/child observe and become aware through discussion of the overt signals in verbal (word usage, intonation, etc) and covert symbols of nonverbal (dress-style, body movement, preferences) communicational patterns of role models exemplifying the four /eight major types of imagoes of the Ethnic Screening Template. This process may be facilitated by providing a graphic word/ visual image picture of the typical ascendent image-symbol in each category.

Ascending/Descending (remission)

Black Male – BM	(positive ntu units)
Black Female – BF	(positive ntu units)
White Male – WM	(positive ntu units)
White Female – WF	(positive ntu units)
Black Male – BM	(negative ntu units)
Black Female – BF	(negative ntu units)
White Male – WM	(negative ntu units)
White Female – WF	(negative ntu units)

Complete Opposites

B.M. (+)	W.F.	(-)
B.F. (+)	W.M.	(-)
B.M. (-)	W.F.	(+)
B.F. (-)	W.F.	(+)

2. Have student/child design attitudinal-value-behavioral-image prescriptions to transform the negative and non-cultural images into positive and cultural images. This may be done through employing a variety of media such as video, rap, poetry, painting, song, dance. etc.
3. Psycho-spiritual-moral principles and Laws to be discussed and internalized during the above exercises.
   a. Laws of attraction, influence and correspondence
   b. Law of enantiodromia (reversal of opposites)
   c. Law of manifestation of energy.

These exercises may be assigned certain ntu-value points (to be explained in later chapter) for various categories and degrees of Self-centered competition and imago-template stage-related maturation. The ntu-points may be assigned on the value of the symbolic form as well as their transfer into the reality context of daily living, family development and community participation.

An outline for the assignment of ntu-Soul Force points is outlined in chapter 16.

Exercise A-2   Monitoring of the relative ntu-value assigned to various images (images build up internally into imagoes) of the eight categories of the ethnic screening template in mass media such as television, radio and magazine.

1. Have student/child bring in pictures and examples of the eight ethnic screening types from various media.
2. Repeat the Transformation exercises listed above.

3. Repeat the discussion of Laws of soul force energy outlined above.

Projections Of the Shadow And Self-Representation

The implications are far reaching with the recognition and correct understanding of the two sets of images and two states of consciousness and the effects on the developing self-concepts and I-dentities of not only Black but White children. Black children, like white children, have a set of Black images that they live and aspire through and they have a set of White images that they live and aspire through.

The correct and proper balance could bring about a healthy wholesome integration of Self. The true inner representational system of Self in Black children has been broken and repressed and has been replaced by a false "ego ideal" schema of Self. The "I" in Black children does not therefore, develop at the rate that is normal for a White middle class child. Self-representation (I-dentity) is central to one's ability to formulate reality and control the different specialized instincts and drives in a manner designed to assure maturation. Self-representation can only occur when all of the internal images of the soul-personality-ego-character-SOUL are striving towards a balanced harmony. The mind becomes attracted to and identified with those images that it spends most of it attention on. Self-concept growing out of the dynamic functioning of the soul-personality-ego-character-SOUL is the organizing force, the glue, which integrates these images along with values, morals, spirituality, space and time into the dynamic reality of an I-dentity that can participate as Co-Creator of Reality.

Self Image Examination

Code 12

BF   WF

BM   WM

Good Ethnic Cultural Self Image-Age 7, Black Female

A. Which one looks like you or resembles you the closest?

Code	Drawing	Sex	Age	Responses
12	BF	F	7	She is black.
32	BM	M	10	He is dark skin.

B. Which one would you like to look like when you grow up?

Code	Drawing	Sex	Age	Responses
12	BF	F	7	She looks better than the other one (WF). Her (WF) legs are like that (gapping) and she is kind of fat.
32	WM	M	10	Because he is light skin.

Code 32

BF  WF

BM  WM

Poor Ethnic Cultural Self Image-Age 10, Black Male

C. Which one is worse in school behavior?

Code	Drawing	Sex	Age	Responses
12	WM	F	7	Cause I messed his clothes up. He just looks like he would be better than the other one. No, I mean worse.
32	BM	M	10	Cause he looks like it. His face looks mean. The color of the face makes him look mean.

D. Which one is worst in school grades?

Code	Drawing	Sex	Age	Responses
12	BM	F	7	He looks bad and I think he would act bad and his hair is crooked.
32	WM	M	10	I dunno.

E. White one is best in school behavior?

Code	Drawing	Sex	Age	Responses
12	BM	F	7	He looks quiet. He looks better than that one(WM).Looks like he would listen to what the teacher say.
32	WM	M	10	He looks nice, he smiles.

F. Which one is the best in school grades?

Code	Drawing	Sex	Age	Responses
12	BF	F	7	I dunno, I just picked her.
32	WM	M	10	He looks like he don't fight nobody. He looks like a nice boy.

G. Which one is happiest?

Code	Drawing	Sex	Age	Responses
12	WM	F	7	This one looks happiest, got the biggest smile maybe happy because he didn't go to another grade. Maybe he just likes to be bad.
32	WM	M	10	Cause he's got a smile on his face. He looks happy. He smiles like he is happy.

H. Which one is saddest?

Code	Drawing	Sex	Age	Responses
12	WF	F	7	Cause her legs are too wide, cause I haven't been choosing her and she is not like the other girl, one of her feet are bigger than the other once. And she thinks that they don't know that she is there.

| 32 | WM | M | 10 | Cause she (he) is not laughing. She (he) got a sad face. She (he) is the only one not laughing. |

I. Which one is weakest?

Code	Drawing	Sex	Age	Responses
12	BF	F	7	She is the smallest. Because girls are not really stronger than boys, the other girl is bigger than her. She looks like a nice girl, so she would want to be strong.
32	WF	M	10	She looks the weakest.

J. Which one is strongest?

Code	Drawing	Sex	Age	Responses
12	WF	F	7	Cause she look like fat, and fat girls are stronger. She has big feet. She doesn't look like she is weak.
32	BM	M	10	He looks like he is strong. His body and his arms look strong.

K. Which one is the ugliest?

Code	Drawing	Sex	Age	Responses
12	WM	F	7	Cause his clothes are all out of shape. His hair is not even, it is black at top and white at bottom. His arms are up. His tie is pulled to suit. He only has four fingers.
32	BM	M	10	Because of the color of his face. Because I put two colors on his face, the orange makes him ugly.

L. Which one is prettiest?

Code	Drawing	Sex	Age	Responses
12	BF	F	7	She has the best clothes. She is not all out of shape like (WM) and her hair is not all out of shape. She has a nice dress.
32	WM	M	10	His face is prettiest, cause his hair on his head—it is combed.

M. Which one most closely resembles your father?

Code	Drawing	Sex	Age	Responses
12	BM	F	7	My father doen't have any hair and they do. My father is much bigger than he.
32	BM	M	10	He is dark. His arms look strong.

N. Which one most closely resembles your Mother?

Code	Drawing	Sex	Age	Responses
12	WF	F	7	This one is skinner and when she goes to work she sometimes wears her hair like that. She looks like she would want to be a nurse, and my mother is mostly smiling like her.
32	BF	M	10	Because of the pants and the sneakers.

O. Which one would you like your father to look in the in the future?

Code	Drawing	Sex	Age	Responses
12	BM	F	7	Cause I would like my father to have more of an Afro like him and not always wear that green jacket every day.
32	BM	M	10	I dunno

P. Which one would you like your mother to look in the future?

Code	Drawing	Sex	Age	Responses
12	BF	F	7	This one looks like her.
32	WF	M	10	Cause she is light skin. Sometimes cause if a black skinned person's face gets dirty he wont see how to get all the dirt off his face but the light skinned people will get the dirt off.

Q. Which one would you like to be a friend?

Code	Drawing	Sex	Age	Responses
12	WF	F	7	She looks like she is a nice girl. She looks like she can fight well.
32	WM	M	10	Because I got a friend light skinned like him. If he found some money he would give me some and if I found some, I would give him some.

R. Which one would you like to be your teacher?

Code	Drawing	Sex	Age	Responses
12	BM	F	7	Men teachers are usually nice. He looks nice. He looks smart and teaches us the right things and gives us the same amount of homework.
32	WF	M	10	We go on trips.

As has been previously mentioned, racial representation and differentiation begins early in the child's growth and maturational process. From the dawning of racial awareness and differentiation, the sense of Self and I-dentity undergoes a developmental progression, regression, confusion, resolution or stasis. Which development racial awareness and differentiation takes depends upon the external and internal feedback that the factor of ethnicity receives in helping the self-concept to structure reality in relationship to the total Self. During this process of development of racial awareness and differentiation of Self, images as well as words and symbols of the invisible template of Self (true or false) becomes operant. The task of the template of Self is to structure the attitudes and cognitive styles that are largely passed on through unconscious, non-verbal and child-rearing practices.

The developing self-concepts of non-mainstream children are further destroyed or enhanced during the child's interaction with the various institutions of society. These institutions program self-concept, sense of self-worth, I-dentity and sense of cultural inclusion-exclusion.

FOR NOTES
Insights, Reflections, Self-Observations

FOR NOTES
Insights, Reflections, Self-Observations

CHAPTER 6:
The Black Hole

Where Do We Go From Here: Chaos Or Community

Without praxis (correct closure), synthesis and an ethical-moral construct (SOUL) to help relate one's various inner components (choices, decisions and actions) to the outer world, the individual is left with a variety of gaps in the soul-personality-ego-character-SOUL structure. These resultant gaps or "lacunae" forever have a regressive, entrophic (the movement towards stasis, inertia and death) pull on the soul-personality-ego-character-SOUL structure of the individual and group. Different individuals react to this regressive, entrophic, backward pull on the soul-personality-ego-character-SOUL in different ways, depending on environmental, socio-economic, temperamental and developmental differences. As these holes of emptiness coalesce, they form lacuna which claim larger and larger segments of the soul-personality-ego-character-SOUL structure and pull it deeper and deeper into the sensuous, material, muddy, "bottomless pit" at both the individual and collective level (family, community, society).

A whole sense of Self-representation and I-dentity can only occur when all of the internal images/imagoes of the soul-personality-ego-character-SOUL are striving towards a balanced harmony in the present moment—the NOW—according to the inner Laws of the Soul. The mind becomes attracted to, and I-dentified with, those images/imagoes that it spends most of its attention on. Self-concept growing out of the dynamic functioning of the soul-personality-ego-character-SOUL is the organizing force, the glue, which integrates these images/imagoes into a coherent whole which negates the gaps or lacunae in the soul-personality-character-SOUL structure. The evolving self-concept is able to incorporate values, morals, spirituality, space and time into the dynamic reality of an I-dentity with Community as Co-Creator of Reality.

Without the self-critical and self-awareness skills that an integrated self-concept and sense of I-dentity affords, there is very little, mostly fragmentary, inner synthesis and integration of the sense of Self. There is little I-magination or image-making ability for constructive, reality-oriented, task-directed behavior. Without this I-mage-I-mago making ability, the individual is not able to create and bring ideas into the Complete Real Stage of the Here and NOW (See diagram).

The Levels of Manifestation of Reality

This is a feed-back circuit and involves the individual in an active, as well as a contemplative phase of activity. This activity involves intervening in the world to create and unfold one's mission and destiny. Without both aspects, active and reflective, of this feedback circuit, praxis or closure is not possible. Here, praxis is used to define "right and balanced actions". Without praxis and closure, the individual is not able to develop a sense of relationship to his/her actions because of tunnel vision, therefore, not able to see in a holistic and ethical manner how these actions affect the environment. This further creates the inner world of fragmentation, isolation, confusion and rejection. Thus, the process of self-destruction continues in its downward spiraling course.

Description Of The Black Hole

The Black Hole is a manifestation of the Shadow, the VOID, the Black Goddess in both her negative and her positive aspects. The positive aspect of the Black Hole represents the urge to cohesion, transformation and Transcendence. The negative aspect of the Black Hole represents the backwards pull unto dissolutionment, chaos, stasis, inertia and self-destructive death. The Black Hole could be visualized as a hurricane. The negative aspect of the Black Hole would be symbolized as the periphery of the Black Hole and the positive would be symbolized as the Eye Of The Storm. The Eye Of The Storm is the safe zone of Transcendence. The Black Hole represents,

Eye of the Storm

collectively, the primal and therefore the denied aspects of ourselves, the secret and unresolved, incomplete aspects of ourselves. These aspects of ourselves are attached to the shadow—the imago-template of Blackness. The negative aspect of the Black Hole collectively represents the holes, the gaps, the lacuna or "empty spaces" that are left from untruthful-unnatural relationships we have established with the Soul, the SELF. Unfortunately, these incomplete and negative associations of Blackness bring about anti-Black cultural sentiments not only among Whites but also among many Blacks and members of other races.

There occurs an ever widening "empty space" in the Collective Soul and conscience of the society and individuals, so eclipsed of a true relation with the positive Shadow, the Soul and imago-template of Blackness. This eclipse causes the individual and the collective to deviate from personal, cultural and moral-spiritual "Center". This refers to both Blacks and Whites. This causes a moral and motivational lassitude which generates anti-Black, anti-Feminine, anti-Spiritual and anti-African cultural sentiments among both Blacks and Whites.

In the Black community, these anti-Black Cultural sentiments are too well demonstrated in the attitudes of indifference, internalized inferiority, nonchalance and ineptitude of many Black businesses and community enterprises. These sentiments are demonstrated so vividly in the backstabbing, "crabs-in-a-barrel" syndrome of many Black community organizations, including churches. It has historically been, and continues, to some extent, to be demonstrated in our Black colleges and universities. These august institutions have often given preferential treatment to the "light-bright and good hair" types among us. These anti-Cultural, anti-Self sentiments reach their tragic heights of manifestation in the phenomenally high Black-on-Black crime rates, child-abuse and property destruction rates which are becoming so common in inner-city African-American communities.

The Oppressive Shadow Of Harlem

Burnt out buildings
blinking blank eyes at bygone tenants
belching fetid, festering fumes
fanned by tepid winds
winding close to the nostrils of weary wanderers.

Dimly lit, dark, dingy, damp hallways
leading to nowhere, nothing
and a never ending sense of nobodiness.
Violence that veers off of vain egos
generating a growing sense of grueling inner pain.
Pee streaming down peopled sidewalks
daring undaunted eyes
that see and do not see.
Noise and nosey neighbors
increase the nameless and numbing sensation
of never-never land.

Try as one may to trot out of this pit
Tramps and thistles
keep one treading and tripping
over trampled tricks
and treasured trails
repeating sadly worn patterns
whose demise should have been mourned long ago.
Trapped in taunt, tight, tension-filled tenements
teeming with totally untamed
and tantalizing realities.
Succored in the seat of the self
by savory images
saturated with stilted, self-separation enzymes.

Verse 12

Especially for us as African-Americans these anti-Black cultural sentiments make it more difficult to properly develop the necessary sentiments of Love, Sharing, Unity and Concern for our own. This lack of Self-Love and Self-Unity results in "holes" or "lacunae" in the soul-personality-ego-character-SOUL of the individual, family and community at the cultural level. Unity and Self-Love of Blackness in all of its manifestations would ensure tighter family and community bonds. These stronger cultural bonds are necessary for the massive cultural upliftment that is critically needed at this time for survival, transformation and transcendence.

The lacuna or the gaps in soul-personality-ego-character-SOUL development in the non-mainstream cultural groups are caused by, and related to, similar gaps in the soul-personality-ego-character-SOUL development of the mainstream cultural group. Both are caused by the deviation from the umbilical connection at the Source, Center and Heart—the SOUL, Mother Africa Within. These gaps in development ever widen and coalease, thereby spelling peril for both groups. The coaleasing of the many lacuna into the collective hole or lacuna would be the archetypal imago-template of CHAOS.

Not until we face and combat this inner psychic strangulation of the archetypal Black-intuitive-feminine "representational system" of Soul, can we begin to fill in these gaps of soul-personality-ego-character-SOUL development of both groups and move toward the synthesis of the opposite—COMMUNITY. This embracing and internalization of the Dark Feminine—the Soul as "vehicle of the living God/Goddess" is necessary in order to stop the spiralling decline of national, cultural, family and personal fragmentation. It is necessary to save us from further in-group conflict, feelings of isolation, unrootedness and unconnectedness.

The Oppressive Shadow Of Harlem

Everybody is looking for somebody
searching in wrong places for any-body.
Possessed by defiant demons
demanding more and more
treading on the unending path of muck, mire and gore.
A face of Harlem glossed over by Madam glory
befreckled with festering frowns
of forgotten fame.
Souls slipping into simpering schemes
of sickening misery and pain
a deep well
of gnawing, nagging, nameless non-identity.
A surrender signaling acceptance
to an assignment of assiduous and aimless death.

Corroded non-caring sensibilities
that caress every fiber of being
deadening and denuding destiny's determination.
Churches on every corner
centered in every block.
Souls searching for salvation
shouting, screeching and screaming
singing of hope, pain and grace
serving as stepping-stones
up the steep climb out of a stagnant existence.

Funeral homes filling up every block
Ship-out shops.
for weary souls
seeking the renamed path
out of their earthly pain.

Verses 10-11

The Passage Of The Sins Of The Parents

These imago-symbolic-complexes serve as the matrix for the transfer of thoughts, attitudes, values and behavioral traits between generations. Through the negative shadowy imago-symbolic-energy complex and its associated "hole" in the conscience, the "sins of the parents are passed on to the children". On many occasions when I have worked long and hard to uncover some resistant trait in a youngster such as stealing or run-away behavior, the final answer came when this trait was discovered to be, or has been, also present in the parent. Many times the trait in the parent has been incompletely resolved or is still present in a veiled or not so veiled way.

In one such case I worked for two years with the teenage son of a middle-class African-American family. This teenager had a severe stealing disorder that had begun to get him into trouble with the law. The father was director of a large youth program and the mother was the principal of the school in her area. After two years the mother revealed that the father had similar stealing traits when he was young. In fact, she revealed that he still would change the price tags on grocery items in the supermarket before reaching the check-out counter. He might also walk out of the store with a pack of cigarettes in his pocket or some other small items. The father was never able to admit to his negative shadowy traits and eventually took his son out of therapy.

Another case in which the shadow is frequently passed from one generation to the next, is in the situation of incest. Often the grown-up victim of incest has not confronted and worked-through this negative shadowy content of her/his soul-personality-ego-character-SOUL. As the females become adults often they are involved in situations in which they allow, knowingly and unknowingly, their daughters to become victimized by their husbands or boyfriends. A vivid case example is that of a 38 y.o. female who was the victim of incest in her childhood but never discussed it until she came into therapy as a result of her three daughters having been sexually abused by their biological father. For two years, this father would, almost nightly, get out of bed with his wife and go into the children's room and awaken the three daughters ranging in ages from 12 to 7. These three girls shared the room with their 4 y.o. brother. This father would make the three daughters go into the living room where he proceeded to have sex with each in term while the others looked on. His vocation was photography and he later began to take pictures of the girls in the nude in the darkroom of the job. On a couple of occasions he took the girls to this studio where he had sex with them and invited a co-worker to have sex with them while he filmed the event. The mother who slept through this for two years had built up a heavy denial, avoidance and evasive imago-symbolic complex related to the denied and repressed incestuous relationship of her past.

These imago-symbolic-complexes often serve as the matrix of influence for symbolic patterns such as stealing, lying, running away, alcoholism and drug abuse. The reason these are often considered symbolic behaviors is because they are signs, symptoms or outward behavioral expressions of deeper unmet, unfulfilled imago-symbolic-complexes. At some time and place during development, the imago-symbolic complexes did not get the necessary and proper nurturance and fulfillment. These inner imago-symbolic complexes are not just limited in their expressions to lags in development. These imago-symbolic-complexes also serve as the matrix for the higher sentiments of human-spiritual evolution, being triggered by the urge of Return to Community.

Besides the outer material objects that the child will encounter and must master during the developmental process, there are internal essences or Soul Forces that will influence the childs I-dentity. These Soul Forces must be internalized, mastered and integrated as functional aspects of the child's soul-personality-ego-character-SOUL. The mother-nurturer and her image-imago and its associated Soul Force is the first and most significant in this early formulation of the sense of Self. These imago-symbolic-energy-complexes are passed between mother and child in the various methods and processes that the mother employs to bond the child. These essences (Soul Forces) are passed on in the mothers' milk, in her eye contact, in her voice, in her touch and, most important, in the early stages of bonding, in her body proximity through holding the baby. In african culture, the practice of tying the baby to the back, signaling the external-uterine stage of gestation, insured that the child's center was in continuous contact with the mother's center during the first two years of the childs' external-uterine development. This proximity of mother's and child's physical centers assured the proximity of their spiritual 'Centers which allowed for the passage of Soul Forces between the two.

During the developmental sequence, the perceptual system (left-brain) involves physical objects as symbols of transferal and attachment of energy. The apperceptual system (right-brain) involves essential (essences) values as symbols of transferal and attachment. If, of course, the imago-symbolic-complex of the mother-feminine is not fulfilled and developed in the mother there will be affect-deficits in how the inner imago-complexes of the child will be developed. Many women who give birth, and live with their children everyday, never become "Mothers". The primary and major imago-complexes of the child that have to be stimulated and developed by the mother are the innerchild-trickster, the feminine-nurturance and to some extent the masculine-will power. Similarly, if the masculine-will power, the feminine-nurturance and the child-trickster are not properly developed in the father, or if father is absent, there will be deficits in how these inner symbolic-energy complexes will be developed in the child.

In a negative-shadowy energy field like the typical inner city Black-Latino community where the Soul has undergone considerable strangulation, every moment of interactive consciousness has to focus on battling with, defending oneself from, trying to overcome, re-educate, rechannel this negative shadowy energy. One forever feels that one is battling against a crumbling dam of energy that threatens to completely devastate one's entire being, life and existence momentarily. This tidal wave of negative shadowy energy creates a perpetual sense of coming-aloose, becoming unbound, becoming unchained—a reversion to the "wilding experience".

One experiences this unchaining phenomenon in one's self and in the masses that one interacts with at various levels. One forever struggles against this sense of becoming bonded to Chaos and dehumanizing dissolutionment. Becoming bonded to Chaos and dehumanizing dissolutionment means becoming bonded, often against one's will to a variety of fragmenting, "wilding", and otherwise impulsive and inner driven behaviors that one seems to have no control over at the time, having temporarily surrender these controls to the inner negative shadowy forces of Chaos. One feels deep down in the depth of one's soul that no amount of laws placed on the books can reverse this dehumanizing process. People without basic Human Rights can never benefit from Civil Rights contained on paper but not practiced. The only staying power that one has of not becoming bonded to the 3/5 human status and "thingness" is the conscious effort that one exerts to patch up the crumbling dam and put the pieces together in an order so that the inundating power by-passes the island that one is steadily etching out, standing on and defending one's self from for the moment. For the masses of African-Americans, this island is outside of the usual supportive systems that a culture and society are supposed to provide for the acculturation of all of its members.

The 3/5 human being as the negative shadow or the "nigger" is the regressive lode-stone in the human soul-personality-ego-character-SOUL structure created by enslavement and destruction of the cultural worldview, I-dentity and group cohesiveness of people of obvious African descent. It is a bonding symbolic energy force that serves as a major Principality of Chaos and dissolution of not only the Black community, but the society at large, if not western civilization. One half of the nigger archetype is in the collective psychic structure of the "invented" 3/5 human race and the other half of the archetype is in the "inventors". Prior to this reduction into the 3/5 human being and its consequences on the development of human consciousness. This oneness of humanity, according to the scholarly work by Martin Bernal—Black Athena, connected and bonded human beings collectively into Mother Africa as the Growing Ancestral Tree and foundational "Pillar" of a human representational worldview.

The Oppressive Shadow Of Harlem

Harlem of the by-gone years
Harlem of past hopes and tears
We call upon the ancestors of the years
to lift us from this veil of fears and tears
Help us regain our ancestral might and Light,
Lead us on to assert our Right and Sight
to be finally and fully who we are
Children of Isis, Woyanga, Horus and Ra.

Verse 13

This group I-dentification with the Ancestral World Tree allowed various cultures to cope with, deal with and transcend the problems and tasks of everyday living and growth in their own way while respecting the integrity of other members of the human family to do the same. When one group declared, for profit motive, that it was their god-given right to dehumanize, exploit and retard the development of another group, the bonding of the human family to the Growing Ancestral World Tree was broken. The Circle became unbalanced. The negative shadow was thus born or at least greatly magnified in the world culture.

The negative shadow affects and influences the attitudes-values-behaviors and paralyzes the moral-ethical structure of all people. This includes both the creators of the nigger or 3/5 human being and those who internalize and live this archetypal symbol. This ranges from the least educated to the most educated and cuts across cultures. This calls to mind a statement by a friend who said "you remember how the Old Folk use to say to us – you can't kill anybody without digging two graves." The negative shadow impairs the skills of the skilled and efficiency of the efficient. It creeps and crawls into one's psychological space like some insidious poisonous gas designed to kill motivation, hope, aspiration, will and industriousness. It taints one's perceptions and reduces one's learned behavioral patterns to half-finished, uncompleted, sloppy attempts at Truth. The negative shadow is a tangled web of sorted sicknesses and weaknesses, including apathy, hopelessness, indifference, projection, anger, lust, greed, avarice, jealousy, doubt, hatred, denial, viciousness, power thirst, avoidance of responsibility and commitment.

Bonding And The Passage Of The Soul Forces

Bonding is necessary to the passage, developmental processes and the nurturance of the "Ancient Properties" within the soul-personality-ego-character-SOUL of the child. These Ancient Properties are referred to in Toni Morrison's book, Tar Baby. The Ancient Properties of the Soul are those timeless, trans-generational, trans-cultural themes that bind the human family together. It is these ancient properties of the Soul that mothering, parenting and the acculturational process in general must pass on to the young.

These ancient properties of the Soul are contained within the essence of the Mandala-Imago-Symbolic-Energy-System-Complexes which comprise the core of the Growing Ancestral World Tree. These ancient properties are passed on to the child through the mothers' milk, touch, eye contact, body warmth, rhythm, voice and childrearing-parenting patterns in general. Thus these ancient properties become imbedded in the unconscious mind and habit traits of the young. These ancient properties are reinforced through ritual tradition and daily routine until they become automatic and autonomous in the collective behavior of the individual and the group. Bonding fosters a sense of belonging, a sense of worth, goodness, love, warmth, unity, wholeness, confidence and trust. The unreflected imago-template of the inner-destructive child of the mother can completely destroy these important elements of bonding in the youngster. An example is the case of a 7 y.o. girl who, out of a sibship of five, is being targeted for abuse by the mother who has a past history of being abused by her mother in her childhood—her inner-child remains in an angry, undeveloped, destructive, unreflected state. The child wakes up with nightmares that her mother is going to kill her or "shoot me with a gun".

Raising of the DJED

Most importantly bonding with the Backbone of one's culture gives a sense of **groundedness, rootedness** and **inclusion**. In ancient Egyptian culture this backbone of culture was referred to as the Tet or Djed. The Tet or Djed was associated with the God of Enlightment—Osiris. The Djed or Tet was symbolized as a tree or trees (double tree) that was ritually erected during the ceremonial season from December through March known as the Raising Of The Djed. It symbolically represented the bonding of the individual with the Ancient Properties of the cultural, moral-spiritual laws embodied in the Egyptian Growing Ancestral World Tree.

Bonding is always necessary to the passage and development of the cultural and racial representational system. It is this cultural representational system which will serve as the context from which the ancient properties of goodness, love, unity and wholeness spring. Within the context of the Backbone, these properties organize themselves and insure their growth and conformity through the structures of consciousness which we have been discussing as the Mandala-Imago-Symbolic-Energy-Complexes.

The inner Mandala-Imago-Symbolic-Energy-System-Complexes or imago-templates are ultimately the compensatory parents. They serve as the inner guardians and mechanisms of inner nurturance for love and all the maturational processes whether real or imagined. These M.I.S.E.S.C. are the ultimate absorbers of stress and strain related to, and generated from, the various relationships that they might attract us into, while seeking their unfoldment and fulfillment. It is ultimately to these inner imago-templates or Soul Forces that we must become bonded.

Words, at some level are synonymous with images. They create images and illusions and build up imagoes that deviate us from this process of deepening our bonds with the Soul Forces as collective Ancient Properties that would bind us into a meaningful cultural relationship with our past and source of Spiritual Power. There is an association of word images that is employed, depending on which of the four schema of the Ethnic Screening Template is in ascendancy (has prominent influence). This association of word images is employed to further shade us from the "Light Of the Pure Land" of the Soul. Each of the imago-templates of the Ethnic Screening Template viewed alone or within the context of the others, is but an illusion, a fragment of the total Reality-the Self, the Indwelling-God.

Currently, as a result of the lack of bonding to the Soul Forces or deeper structures of consciousness and the resultant expanding lacuna or gaps in conscience in the collective Soul of America, families both in and out of the mainstream, are undergoing a de-centering, foundation-shaking crisis. This crisis is affecting all classes and ages, especially the young and signal a descent into the archetype of Chaos at the collective national level. More specifically, and more to our immediate concern, are the families out-of-the-mainstream. As a result of the lack of bonding to these deeper inner structures of consciousness and the resultant fragmentation of the inner, cultural, Soul-centered filter of Self and the loss of the Ancient Properties, it is difficult for the new generation of non-mainstream and mainstream youngsters to experience continuity with their past and with themselves.

African-Americans and Africa-Carribeans as cultural groups have made few definitive plans and have established few cultural institutions to affirm, validate and integrate this intuitive, Soul-centered worldview of Ancient Properties into their daily lives. Therefore, there has been no ample replacement of the filtering template that the revolutions of the sixties broke—(The White/European/Superiority

Template). In the absence of not having consciously developed or strengthened an Africentric culture-centered "yoking and binding" system of Ancient Properties, many of these groups have thrown off the yoke of oppression only to re-internalize it under some ego-syntonic pseudonym. The inapplicability and virulence of these non-cultural, oppressive, align images, symbols and beliefs continue, many times, in their deceptive pseudo-cultural state with redoubled consequences. They perpetually attract the African-American. if not all Americans, away from their true center—the Heart of SOUL, in search of unrealistic dreams and unfulfillable expectations.

The crisis and the task at hand is the return to center or the "Return To The Source" which will involve closing of the gaps and the closing of the Temple of Janus. Janus is the two headed God which looks in both directions and in many ways represents the gaps between the two worldviews—material/spiritual, Western/African, and White/Black. The process of centering depends largely on the alignment of the two wills. The small or conscious will governs life-style issues. The act of centroversion (returning to the Spiritual-Transcendental Center—aligning with the Great Mother and her Ancient Properties) depends on submission to the greater spiritual WILL from the "yoking center" of the Life-Track.

Exercises In Closing The Gaps

Lack of closure (not putting a close on things, completion) adds to the regressive backward flowing, negative aspect of the Black Hole.

Projects left unfinished and uncompleted, have a regressive, draining effect on the Soul Force of not only the individual, but the collective Community. These holes or lacuna act as psychic-energy leeches to drain the Soul Force or Vital Force from the individual or the collective.

The Oppressive Shadow Of Harlem

People with stooped shoulders and staggering gaits
swaying under an invisible sweltering heat of oppression
that short-circuits the mind saturates the body
and saps the spirit.
Elderly people, peering out of propped-up windows
appraising shadowy appearances of youth
unappealing in their imprisonment,
fatal in their designs.

Droopy dogs
dropping more than fleas
as they drag from place to place
to doze in the shade.

Noise boxes blasting and booming
like bickering beams
bottled in a bound vacuum
of taunt anxieties,
causing trauma to tender nerves
and already trammelled souls.

Bums and bag-ladies
bumping into by-passers
blinded by binding inner mutterings
musing at the mind.

Verses 8-9

The goal of development for all individuals, Black as well as White, is to embody (live) a harmonious balance of these inner imagoes of the self. Both the primal images of Blackness and those of Whiteness must be integrated as positive without ignoring their negatives—to create a whole person(ality).

In order to bring about closure, the conscious will has to make choices, decisions, actions and changes (C.D.A.C.) in order to complete the various tasks of inner integration, development and maturation.

The inner infinite and everlasting entity of the Soul's Life-Track interspheres through choice, consciousness and will, with the outer (material) world of various life-styles. We exist in both inner and outer worlds at all times. While there is a part of us that is solving problems and growing in the material world, there is also a part of us that is solving problems and growing in the inner spiritual/archetypal world. We work on the problems of growth and maturation on many different levels at one time. These levels include the spiritual, mental, emotional and physical which encompasses the eleven levels of the imago-templates.

Conscious will-to-choose and participational acts to concretize those choices, are the basis of transcendence and Self-Realizing behaviors. The rite of choosing and Being is characterized by the transformative formula of choice, decision, action and change (C.D.A.C.). With repeated application and internalization of this formula, the conscious will meshes with the Divine Will in the Covenant of Truth, Duty, Praxis and Dharma (T.D.P.D.). Unlike the rest of nature, we do have a choice partially over which symbols we will and will not allow to express in and through us as vehicles.

C.D.A.C--T.D.P.D Diagram

(C.D.A.C.) Exercises

List Seven Projects that you as an individual and/or group have started and not finished.

1.
2.
3.
4.
5.
6.
7.

List those that can be recovered from the Black Hole of oblivion.

1.
2.
3.
4.
5.
6.
7.

List the Choices, decisions and actions necessary to salvage those projects that can be salvaged.

    a.

    b.

    c.

List some of the dynamics at the individual and the collective (family, community, group) level that contributed to the above lack of closure on the: projects outlined.

    1.

    2.

    3.

    4.

    5.

    6.

    7.

List the various realms that lack of closure on the above dynamics belong at the

    a.   Physical
    b.   emotional
    c.   mental-intellectual
    d.   spiritual-moral

How the Law of Karma is related to the Dynamics of the Black Hole.

How are the archetypes of Chaos and Community as outlined by Martin Luther King, Jr. related to the negative and the positive aspects of the Black Hole?

Ways of strengthening the Soul to resist the negative dynamics of the Black Hole and employing the dynamics of the Black Hole as a transformative experience:

1. Talking correctly—using speech to affirm not destroy. Resist talking negatively about people and situations.
2. Martial arts, dance, jogging, aerobic exercises and other physical disciplines to assist a disciplined integration of body, mind and soul.
3. Relaxation, meditation and visualization to perform the inner work of strengthening the imaginal, invisible self.
4. Practice of right relations, right attitudes, right behavior, right values to insure harmonious interactions with other people, things and nature.
5. prayer.
6. Correct diet.
7. Correct actions designed to assure growth and maturation.

FOR NOTES
Insights, Reflections, Self-Observations

CHAPTER 7:
The Doctrine of the Two Minds

The doctrine of the two minds (the two modes of cognition), simplistically states that there has always been two minds. One mind or mode of cognition has its center in the heart (right-brain mode) and the other has its center in the brain (left-brain mode). All people of all cultures employ both modes of cognition but frequently individuals and cultures have a predominant mode.

The goal of the maturational process is to develop a healthy balance and integration of both modes. In ancient Egypt the dominant mode was the spiritual-intuitive-rational mode which allowed for the development of one of the highest cultures the world has ever known. This spiritual-intuitive-rational mode with its heart centeredness was symbolized in Egyptian art and symbols by showing the people always stepping off on the left foot. So in just about all early Egyptian drawings, the left foot is extended. As the culture began to be dominated by invaders such as the Greeks and Romans, there occurred a transition in the art symbols to mark the transition in philosophy, worldview and cognitive style. In Egyptian art of the Greek and Roman period, the people are characteristically shown as stepping off on the right foot. This represents a shift to left-brain dominance in cultural worldview. The left brain controls the right side of the body below the neck. The right-brain controls the left-side of the body below the neck.

When any dominant mode (right or left brain) in ascendancy is over utilized to the suppression and exclusion of other modes-these other modes tend to become inaccessible to the conscious mind. When they become inaccessible to the conscious mind (in descendance), they begin to set up compensatory methods of re-entering consciousness—ofttimes by storm, or a take over of the mind. In many cases this "storming of the mind" by unconscious contents can be negative and even dangerous. By whatever means these unconscious contents seek to regain consciousness, the movement is referred to as the "return of the repressed". This return of the repressed is also known in psychological and mythological tradition as an "enantiodromia" or "swinging in the opposite direction"—the pendulum swings in the opposite direction when its momentum has been spent in a certain direction.

The Return of the Shadow

The Swinging of the Pendulum
The Return of the Repressed

A Soul-Centered philosophy and worldview (representational system) is all important in labelling and naming the context of an Africentric cultural worldview that has been repressed and neglected. This ancient and timeless Self-representational system is re-emerging as the Mandala of the Dark Feminine—The Soul. This book is an attempt to put some of the philosophical and symbolic concepts of

Soul culture on a concrete level so that they can be better applied to daily living, child-rearing practices and family-community development. By so doing, we assist the re-integration of the Dark Mother—The Soul.

The dominant culture of America systematically prevents the establishment of this inner, integrated and coherent sense of Self in African-Americans. By denying this sense of Soul-Identity to African-Americans, European culture denies a most important component of its own earlier I-dentity rooted in the African origins of all humanity. The dominant Eurocentric culture carries out this repression through conscious, systematic suppression of the right-brained mode, the spiritual-rational mode of knowing ourselves and reality. The mainstream culture valuates the intuitive mode of cognition as less than human. The dominant mainstream culture consequently treats African-Americans in a less-than-human manner. The European cultural representational system (the left-brain, rational-logical mode) has been espoused as the only true mode of knowing reality and knowing the self. Therefore, it is embedded in the minds, through subliminal images and symbols, with intent and outcome of affecting us from the cradle to the grave. These suppressive attempts consequently have served to repress and suppress other modes of knowing reality and the Self that are equally or even more valid for true cognition. The European-American representational system has replaced this more valid and superior mode of cognition of the heart and Soul.

The Soul and its forces, after being held under repression over the past two thousand or so years, is seeking re-integration into consciousness. This re-integration is occurring on many different levels at one time and need our conscious assistance.

These Soul Forces or imago-templates form the Growing Ancestral World Tree, which if not integrated in our development, remains outside of us (individually and collectively) and grows against us.

These intuitive-symbolic "Soul Forces" of the unconscious mind and natural environment persist in an unintegrated and often disruptive manner today in the behavior of Westerners, including African-Americans. Without a proper value frame of reference or representational system of SOUL, these unintegrated natural forces of the Soul find distorted means of expression in and through our daily attitudes-values and behaviors. Further molded and distorted by an oppressive society that has practiced the most inhumane forms of punishments to keep them repressed, these unintegrated Soul Forces are reaching pathological proportions in what we refer today as the Negative Self-Concept Syndrome.

According to recent research findings in Bi-cognitive theory (Right Brain-Left Brain theory), the right-brain, the old brain, the passive-feminine brain, seems to have an "edge" of superiority over the masculine, left brain mode of cognition and consciousness. This research is well documented in Goldberg's book: The Intuitive Edge. The right-brain mode of cognition (knowing of reality) is related more to the development of human consciousness in its earlier African-Eastern stages of growth, development and maturation. It is this intuitive mode that is now returning and taking center-stage in human development and consciousness. The "Return of the Repressed" or the "Return of the Mother" represents a return of the symbolic-intuitive forces. This return has been spoken of variously throughout literature, whether in the sciences, arts, humanities, government, as the "return of the shadow" or the "re-integration of the symbolic", "the awakening of the sleeping dragon", etc.

The return of the repressed intuitive energies of the Dark feminine—the Soul—is an inner urge to communal growth which is being expressed at both the individual and the collective levels. The same laws of inner growth applies whether it is the individual or the collective that is called to inner growth and I-dentification with the Higher SOUL. We are all intimately and inextricably interwoven and interconnected in the I-dentity of the One Transcendent Body-the inner Beloved Community. This call to communal growth is a process of healing or re-en-Souling the earth.

The First Test at the First Gate
The Negative Shadow

As one searches for the Soul, one encounters certain barriers which serve as tests to strengthen one's will-power and resolve to find the Soul/Self—to unveil the Goddess. These barriers and tests come

from that part of the Soul that one encounters first as one "takes up the path"—namely the negative shadow. These tests vary in intensity, degree, timing and specificity. They are designed to test and strengthen soul-personality-ego-character weaknesses from a Karmic, developmental, characterological point of view whether of the individual-family-cultural-societal Self. As one searches, one must be ready to encounter the other aspects of the Self in their blissful tendencies as well as their decadent tendencies. This is not only true of individuals but of groups and societies as well. The encounters with the Soul can be relatively innocuous as well as extremely dangerous. For according to Hannah,

> "The first figure we usually meet in the confrontation with the unconscious is the personal shadow. Since (s)he mainly consists of what we have rejected in ourselves, (s)he is usually quite uncongenial to...".

She also states:

> "It may be difficult for the unprepared reader to understand why facing the unknown in ourselves is a 'dangerous' enterprise. Only experience can teach one

what a terrifying enterprise it is to turn away from the familiar affairs of our conscious world and face the entirely unknown in the inner, unconscious world".

Fear and panic of the terrible contents of the inner world, the negative shadow, are the first to be confronted and must be subdued before the journey into the Self can be resumed, at the individual, as well as, at the societal level. At the societal level, the inner city ghetto experience is the neglected, negative, shadowy aspect of national character-soul development. There is a living, pulsating shadow of unknowing that hovers over ever ghetto experience no matter where that experience takes place in space and time.

The Oppressive Shadow of Harlem

Darkened dreams
dangling from damaged minds
daunted hopes, done
in by dangerous designs
employing deadly,
deeply disturbing images.

Momma's boys
begging, borrowing and breaking laws
basking in the sun with beaded balls of sweat,
having fun
high off of heavenly hash, dust, downs
and other drugs
that are dutifully done.

marijuana smoking,
cocaine-toting people
looking with disdain on heroin addicts
stooping, swaggering and staggering
up the chilled slopes of death.

Drug pushers

shooting at shoddy; shipwrecked sailors
sailing on a sinister sea of shameless sinfulness
in search of sunken treasures
covered over with slime
slithering from insipid sangrenous caverns of the mind.

People cringing from criminal assaults
carried out in places
where the "cream of the crop"
refuse commerce.
Crimes of passion, greed and gore
feeding a satiety that is never satisfied
but always thirsting, lusting for more.

Soul-owned shops
that set up to shut down
without having shaped up
saddled with sorrowfully slumping sales
assisted by finagling fingers
and tales told tailored to deceive.

Verses 1-3 I

It is these largely unintegrated forces of the unconscious mind that influence not only Black but also White society. They influence white society from their repressed and denied African origins as well as through all the attributes that the latter society steals from Black culture without validating the Source.

The Oppressive Shadow Of Harlem

Patterns of oppression pressing tightly against the mind,
squeezing and squashing whatever squints of motivation
that dare to squirm in the realm of conscious will.
Minds programed by self-hate
hastily heaped upon high hopes of reaching heights
of self-discovery.

Pimps, prostitutes and punks
pushing their punished wares on pleasure possessed people
passing through peopled places
panting with passion
pinning for possible charges of more.

Verse 6

The Soul sets certain tasks for the personality-ego-character to solve. These are necessary tasks for the evolvement and unfoldment of the soul-personality-ego-character-SOUL of the individual and the society. There are different and more complex tests at the successive levels of psycho-spiritual development and soul-personality-ego-character-SOUL individuation.

Passing the Tests at the Seven Gates
The Evolving Wisdom Of The Soul

The wisdom of the Soul comes through self-observation and truthful Self-correction at the eleven different imago-template levels of development and maturation. Self is observed in its larger, extended aspects; how it relates to, and gets feedback from, the environment, i.e.: people, plants, books, animals, inanimate objects, etc. This wisdom from within leads to consciousness of the unity of the Soul with all things and all processes within and without.

Consciousness is the ability to experience the Self as SOUL in its fuller extensions and ramification. It is the ability to experience the Oneness, the Harmony and the Unity of the Unified Field of Energy—God. It involves being in touch with the Universal Mind.

Human beings are unique in that they are intermediaries of the forces of nature and the universe. They are creative beings who are immersed in and can consciously utilize the forces that the "Unified Field", "Ground", "Sphere", "Source" or "Prima Materia" of energy. This "Source" represents the "Dark Feminine". The question and the task at hand is how to become more aware of, align with, and better utilize the energies of the "emerging Dark Feminine"—the Soul as Ground of Being.

Through the ego's constant interaction and participation in this re-aligning experience with the Soul which at this level is represented to us as semi-real, we are able to bring ideas, symbols, sentiments and concepts of this cultural cognitive style into concrete Material Realization (Complete-Real). The creativity of human beings which resides in their soul-personality-ego-character-SOUL is an aspect of the Self which ultimately is one of the highest levels of schema (patterns of inner organization of reality) in relationships. This creative "gift" of Spirit which Black Folk have, is rooted in biological inheritance and is either enhanced or hampered, and even destroyed, depending on the individual's interactions with the environment.

Creativity promotes the survival of the species and aids the person's adaptation to the environment. Everyone is a Creator to some extent except those who have completely given up on life and have begun the withdrawal into the long silence of death. Enslavement and continued repression and suppression of our intuitive-spiritual worldview has been, and continues to be, a masterplan to destroy our creativity, our inner Horus-Christ-Ori-Light, and assign us to the realm of death whether physically or psychologically.

The Choice of Community Over Chaos

If this new "returning" spiritual energy is filtered through the africentric system, which is a preserved, somewhat well organized and scientific symbolic system of Transcendence, there is more of a possibility for proper development and correct guidance of these Soul Force energies. Proper guidance of these returning Soul Force Energies is important as they move us collectively into the formation of the One Transcendent Body of Community.

Within this One Transcendent Body, growth and individuation of one affects the growth and individuation of all. The One Transcendent Body is "Awakened Consciousness" in the collective human psyche. This awakened consciousness is working its materialization and manifestation outward from the deep recesses of our Souls as we are called to join the One Great Soul. No one transforms or is transformed in isolation. The "prima materia" of personal transformation is as much in the outer world and the collective as it is in the inner world and the individual self. The Symbolic Energy Systems (Soul Forces) integrate the two. The orisha/archetypes (imago-templates) are different personifications or symbolizations of the "prima materia". They are organizing forces/patterns that guide the evolutionary, developmental process of consciousness and insure the orderly progression, creative transformation and transcendence of one form and "state of being" over another. They guide the return of the repressed and its proper re-integration into human consciousness.

Even though all Soul Forces are considered as belonging to the Great Feminine or unconscious mind, many of them are predominantly male in characteristics. Most Soul Forces have a dominant aspect either male or female, but usually contain the opposite sexual aspect also. All Soul Forces have potentials to be both good and evil. This depends upon how they are approached by the conscious mind and behavior. These Soul Forces are symbolic forces of the unconscious mind/Soul that must be integrated in order for humans to live harmoniously with the invisible and non-human world. These invisible and non-human natural aspects of our environment make up important components of the One Transcendent Community Of Self.

Black people awaken and activate the Soul Forces of the unconscious mind though their natural rhythm. With their body motion, they infuse everything they touch with a "Soul Force", a vibration which is infectious and which could be the saving grace of America.

Blacks are better able to handle these inner contents of the Soul than Whites, since Blacks have culturally kept more in touch with them. However, without a proper value frame of reference or representational system, they find distorted means of expression by both Whites and Blacks alike. Further, molded and distorted by an oppressive society that has practiced the most inhuman forms of repression, their expression reaches pathological proportions in both the Black and White societies with unparalleled cases of obsessive, compulsive, bizarre, psychotic, possessed, dissociative states of behavior. The pathological development of these inner forces is reaching crisis proportions in what we refer today as the Negative Self-Concept Syndrome. This syndrome is a cluster of negative obsessive, compulsive behaviors-attitudes-values which are associated with Blackness in its negative aspect.. This syndrome reaches neurotic, dissociative and psychotic proportions at times.

The purpose of participation in the Orisha/Archetypal/Soul Forces is to allow one to undergo the mystic transformation of maturation and development. This mystic transformation assures the process of ever-widening the limits of human consciousness until one participates readily in the Divine Forces. When one is harmonized with the natural forces of his/her Soul Forces/Orisha, things flow more harmoniously. When one gets out of harmony with these inner natural forces, things begin to go badly, either at the psychological, physical, material or spiritual levels.

The mission of more conscious participation in the archetypal/ Orisha/Soul Forces is to transform and/or translate the Soul Forces of the Inner-Self. Instead of pathologically expressing these forces they should be sublimated into creative, transformative forces to shape the environment.

The mission of more conscious participation in the archetypal/ Orisha/Soul Forces is to transform and/or translate the Soul Forces of the unconscious mind into creative transformative forces to shape the Self and environment into one harmonious whole Being. The Soul Forces constitute both the "Shadow" and the "Spirit Of Enlightment" in human behavior. The Soul Forces represent the evolutionary urge, the driving instincts of nature that propel life ever forward with the tendency to organize as it advances. They communicate through the intuitive process of the right-brain and serve as the core around which all knowledge and experience is organized. It is in and through these forces that the higher psychic (psi) abilities are expressed. Their expressions are known to us as the "inner voices", "the still small voice within", "the voice of the silence", "Inner promptings". They include such communications as pre-cognitive experiences, premonitory experiences, far visions, astral travel, dreams, instincts, drives and urges.

Through their interrelations and interactions, the Soul Forces create rapport, synchronicity, and harmony. They are capable of creating disharmony, mental and physical illness. They are involved with the essence and value relations which we find through the right-brain mode of cognition. It is the task of all people at all times to re-integrate the instinctual, natural forces of the Soul (unconscious mind). This re-integration of the Soul and its forces is not only necessary for a balanced healthy mind, but imperative for the survival of the species. This process has been variously described in psychology and religion as the "Return To The Mother", a process of "mystic transformation" that allows humans to know and participate in the spiritual-rational functions of the "Realm of the Gods".

In the traditional Soul-Centered worldview of people of African descent, God, the natural forces (Deities, Gods) and ancestral spirits, inform the ethics, aesthetics, values and creative expressions that guide the cognitive processes of not only everyday, but transcendental living in the Community Of Oneness.

Passages of Initiation

Transformations of Self Initiation

(Making the transition and transformation from a material-centered reality to Spiritual-Centered Reality)

Moving past Objects (the material) to Essence (the spiritual).

Moving past Existing (centered in material reality) to Being (centered in spiritual reality).

Moving past Apathy to Hoping.

Moving past Chance to Scoping (intuitively assessing a situation before deciding to act).

Moving past Hate to Love.

Moving past Dependency to Responsibility.

Moving past Group Acceptance (outer focused acceptance) to Self Acceptance (inner focused acceptance).

Moving past Selfishness to Selflessness.

Moving past Lying to Truth.

Moving past Cruelty to Nurturance.

Moving past Wrongful Pride to Humility.

Moving past Greed to Generosity.

Moving past Instability to Stability.

Moving past Ignorance to Knowledge.

FOR NOTES
Insights, Reflections, Self-Observations

CHAPTER 8:

The Finding of the Soul

Traditionally, people of non-mainstream cultural groups have been and continue to be strongly influenced by the "Soul" as a healing model. This is especially true of those cultural and ethnic groups which have kept alive their ancestral ties to Mother Africa. This also applies to those cultural groups which have kept alive their spiritual tradition in relation to Mother Nature and the Invisible Forces.

The Soul as a representational worldview and healing system is composed of a central "Vital Force" which includes God at the center and apex. Further it includes nature deities, ancestral spirits and other invisible, unseen intelligent forces of the innerself. The belief in the Soul as the representational worldview of Africentric people has survived down through the centuries. This belief does not differ significantly from such western psychological concepts as "collective unconscious mind", "archetypes" and "autonomous complexes".

These practices and beliefs, inherent in the representational worldview of Soul, serve as the foundational format, the Ancient Properties or imago-templates of Black culture. These imago-templates serve the purpose of inner spiritual organization, outer material manifestation and transcendent symbolization and Self-Realization. Transcendent symbolization refers to the ability to go beyond the odds of physical limitations and the logical-rational choices of the moment. The act of transcendence relies upon a unique characteristic of the individual's ability, through faith, to tap and utilize invisible forces and powers to "make things happen" or to "call forth" things into being/BEING. In a recent interview with a grandmother trying to raise three rebellious grandsons inherited from her crack-addicted daughter, the grandmother said "I feel that I have fallen from Grace. I used to be able to call forth things and now nothing seems to go right. I have lost that power." I automatically knew that this ability to "call forth things" referred to the spiritual powers of the underlying Soul-culture in which she had a strong, even if unstated belief.

This ability to call forth and make things happen is called "Ache" in the Yoruba culture of West Africa and in the African culture of the diaspora. Essentially, this grandmother's statement was a testimony that she was feeling un-rooted and un-connected to an inner spiritual source of Power that she believed in and once was more in touch with.

The Soul as a living, intelligent "entity" or Life-Track phenomenon has passed down through the centuries and generations as a current or stream of consciousness. This stream of consciousness has foroughed deeper and deeper from the body of the collective conscious mind of the race. This has occurred as a result of two interrelated dynamics. First it has occurred because of the dominant cultures' attempt to overtly destroy this dark, feminine, spiritual undercurrent of Africentric culture—it's Heart of Soul. Secondly, it has occurred as a result of the masses of Black peoples' over-identification with the dominant culture and subsequently viewing this "entity" of Soul as a negative feature to be repressed. Many African-Americans, as many Africans, like Europeans, can only tolerate the concept of Soul in their music, their dance, sex and other physical expressions.

Despite numerous attempts at repressing and destroying this "Soul" entity of non-mainstream cultural groups, it still persists just under the surface of consciousness. This Soul entity has undergone many transformations, transmutations and sublimations. Today it is resurfacing in redoubled strength primarily, and paradoxically, as a result of two movements in the scientific realm. First, is the current scientific revolution in split-brain research with the consequent development of the "bi-cognitive" or "left-right brain" theories. Roger Sperry and others are widely known for their innovative research in this area. Second, is the recent findings and theories in molecular physics. Even though this Soul entity has been predominantly in the background of the lives of Black people, it has persistently determined so many of their overt, foreground daily attitudes-values-behaviors at all levels of functioning.

The Soul is the "Ground of Being" of the Africentric worldview and is the womb from which the physical body, emotions, and intellect arise. The Soul is motivated by, and kept alive by, an energy called "Vital Force" or "Spirit." This inner force of the Soul is also called "Soul Force".

The Soul is immortal. This means that it continues to grow through time and space and continues after death, or even after the physical body is no longer in existence. The body is said to be, according to the ancient Egyptian tradition, the "net" of the Soul. The Soul is enmeshed in the desires and material constraints of the body (physical, emotional and mental), from which it must ultimately free itself.

According to Barbara Hanna, a noted Jungian analyst, in her book **Encounters With The Soul: Active Imagination** this inner spiritual world of the Soul is more real and lasting than the outer world. The communications from this inner world come as the Voice of the Symbol. These communicative voices and messages of the symbols usually appear suddenly from the inner depths of the Soul. They appear as inner guidance through intuitions, insights, dreams, revelations, precognition and other phenomena. These intuitive messages from the innerself come in a variety of circumstances. These circumstances vary from silent meditation to moments of intense activity. These inner intuitive communications are transmitted through a variety of mediums such as Orisha-archetypal-ancestral spirit forms which are triggered by, and enhanced by, certain ritual practices and widely held belief in Black and other non-mainstream cultural groups.

The goal of the study of psyche (Soul) was to bring about inner integration of the lower self with the Higher Self and ultimately, At-One-Ment with the Source. The Science of the Soul has been kept alive and passed down through the ages in the traditions of initiation. The discipline of psychology that westerners are familiar with, far from being a science, does not even include the Soul. This modern material-Eurocentric psychology serves as the outer cover of something much deeper-the transcendent model of the Soul.

Our ancestors were wise enough to incorporate many of the most important and central ideas, beliefs and practices of initiation and transcendence, at the heart and core of the external belief systems (religion, psychology, philosophy, education) of various cultures. For instance many of the symbols of initiation are intricately and inextricably intertwined with Catholic tradition, ritual practices and initiatory rites. These initiatory symbols and themes are more overtly employed in the Masonic rites and in the Rosicrusian rites and beliefs. They run throughout Buddhist, Hindu, Taoist, American Indian, Polynesian, Asian and other belief systems. They are obviously celebrated as the core of such initiatory belief systems as the Yoruba, Santeria, Macuumba, Condonble, Voudou, Lucumi and other systems with direct African connections.

This high Science of inner transformation of the soul-personality-ego-character-SOUL is the original science of "psyche". Perhaps in its highest known form, this science was practiced in the ancient Egyptian culture-the birth place of Greek-Roman-Judaeo-christian religious beliefs and modern Western psychology. For many reasons modern psychology has deviated from this inner science of psyche and has become entrenched and entrapped in a materialistic science.

Today the science of psychology, which is an ego-centered psychology, is no longer a science of the Soul. Nor does the present day psychological model include the "children of the soul" as descendants of those who were originally in possession of the advance Science of Soul. This deviation from psyche as the All-Inclusionary Model has done damage to the development of modern humankind; not just Africentric people. Modern humanity is in search of its Soul and if it doesn't hurry and find it, there will be little need for it.

The true template of the self-the Soul—is the Individuated Self. This true Self stands in dynamic opposition to, and is the reverse aspect of, the reality of the WRSC/BNSSC Template of self. "The Self as Soul-Centered" constitutes the true template of Self of all human beings and is the template of the individuated, perfected Self which is Indwelling. The Individuated SELF is represented as the full development of the soul-personality-ego-character-SOUL—the Ori,--the LIGHT. This Light has been reflected in great world leaders, at the real and/or symbolic level, down through the ages in such Archetypal figures as Jesus the Christ, Horus, Hathor, Ra, Isis, Buddha and others. These are models of the fully Self-Realized Being—The En-Souled Being—The Divine Being—The Beloved Community.

The Ethnic Screening Template as the false dominant, ego-centered, eclipsing template of Self, operates predominantly from the rational, material-centered, masculine-oriented, left-brain. In comparison, the original-True Template of Self operates predominantly from the intuitive, spiritual-centered right-brain. These templates affect the person from birth to the grave in their representation of self/not-self, desirability/undesirability, lovability/unlovability, self-worth, self-esteem, self-concept and identity/non-identity.

The Soul Consists of Two Major Divisions

- The central organizing, unifying nucleus which is the soul-personality-ego-character-ego-SOUL. It has a divine core of consciousness called in Yoruba tradition, "the Ori," or Indweller. In Judeao Christian tradition, this would be called the indwelling "Christ". In other traditions it is referred to as Hidden Indweller. Animal, plants and all things, even stones, have their Soul and their Ori.

- The accidental faculties (desires, affects, intellect) through which the Soul experiences life and reality. There are seven major levels and three-sub-levels of accidental faculties which we shall call the Imago/Symbolic/Energy System Complexes or Soul Forces. The seven major levels of Symbolic I-mago-complexes cover the major **life-experience areas** that the self must be initiated into, go through and grow through in order to mature and become Self-Realized. Each of the accidental faculties are but veils of illusions and extensions of the one central and all-encompassing SELF. These Imago-Symbolic-

97

Energy System Complexs will be discussed more fully in a later chapter.

The Seven Imago-Symbolic-Energy-Systems of the Soul-Personality-Ego-Character- SOUL are:

Level	VII	self, christ, buddha, isis—fourth Level of the Spiritual
Level	VI	hero (ine)—third Level of the Spiritual
Level	V	ancestral World Tree—second Level of the Spiritual
Level	IV	love—higher Mental—lower Spiritual
Level	III	paternal/male/masculine/will Power—lower Mental
Level	II	maternal/female/feminine/nurturance—emotional
Level	I	child/trickster/path finder/fool—physical
Pre-level	I	The False Shadow, The Ethnic Screening Template
Pre-level	II	the Indwelling Light
Pre-level	III	The 'the Ground of Being" The Unknown, The Interphase, The Positive Shadow, The Womb of The Dark Mother.
Level	XI	The Integrator—the soul-personality-ego-Character-SOUL is the synthesis and summation of the other ten levels.

Simple Definitions and Descriptions of the Soul for Teaching and Parenting Purposes

The following are actual associations and definitions of the Soul produced by youngsters of various ages during group or individual sessions.

1. The Soul is the Inner Self—the invisible world inside of you. It is the Divine, Spiritual "You" inside of yourself.

2. The Soul expresses itself in feelings, attitudes and desires both negative and positive.

3. After your physical body has gone, the Soul is what's left—According to the teachings of the ancient Egyptians, the "Body is the (ka) of the Soul." The body is the vehicle of the Soul.

4. The Soul expresses itself when you are happy and constructive and it comes out. This is the positive aspect of the Soul. The Soul also expresses itself when you are angry and Destructive and it comes out. This is the negative aspect of the Soul.

5. The soul is the vehicle for learning, memory and experience.

6. The Soul is relationships and expresses itself in how we relate to each other.

7. The Soul expresses itself through intuition, dreams and other symbolic ways.

8. The Strong Soul enables us to cope and handle the stresses of bad situations. The Strong Soul helps us to get along with others in a constructive and healthy manner.

9. The Soul is the Organ of Union between the body and the Spirit.

10. The Soul is continuous with our personality-ego-character.

11. The Soul is the vehicle of memory and experience. As such, it is the record of chronic habit patterns. Therefore, there is a constructive aspect and a destructive aspect of the Soul.

12. The Soul is guided and developed by the process of attention.

13. The Soul is constantly vigilant and is continuously in the process of constructing new schema (habit patterns) of behavior and destroying others, even during sleep.

14. The Soul operates on the principles of Harmony, Rhythm and Cyclic Change.

15. Ways of strengthening the Soul:

1. Talking correctly—using speech to affirm not destroy. Resist talking negatively about people and situations.
2. Tae Kwon-Do or other disciplines designed to assist a disciplined integration of body, mind and soul.
3. Relaxation, meditation and visualization to perform the inner work of strengthening the imaginal, invisible self.
4. Practice of right relations, right attitudes, right behavior, right values to insure harmonious interactions with other people, things and nature.
5. Prayer
6. Correct diet
7. Correct actions designed to assure growth and maturation.

Principles of the Soul

1. All things are of One Essence—The Soul (Ori) Essence.
2. The Universal Mind Of God is the only creator, everything is created through the mind/Soul of God.
3. Our Higher Souls/minds correspond to the Soul/mind of God. We are co-creators of our present state of affairs. We can help determine our fate by our force of thoughts, decisions, actions and habits.

Sentence Completion Exercises

1. My Soul is _____

   _____

2. My Soul helps me to_____

   _____

3. My Soul came from _____

   _____

4. When I die, my Soul goes_____

   _____

5. The "good voice" of my Soul sometimes tell me to____

   _____

6. The "bad voice" of my Soul sometimes tell me to_____

_____

Soul-Centered Teachings for Children

SOUL:

That part of the Self that goes up to God when you die. It is the battery inside of you, it is the battery that charges your heart.

FUNCTIONS:

It helps us to grow mentally, psychologically and spiritually in time and space.

It makes us work.

It charges our body.

It has a positive, a negative, and a neutral-middle aspect.

It serves as a memory book for right and wrong actions as well as relationships. It serves in the development of Ache (Soul-Force) which is the power necessary to fuel the journey of the quest for the Jewel In the Lotus (The Essence of the True Self).

Blocks to the Harmony of the Soul

1. Evil Thoughts
2. Negative Thoughts
3. Insecure thoughts
4. Weaknesses
5. Wrong Actions
6. Wrong Relationships
7. Wrong Words
8. Wrong Attitudes

Full Moon Song

Mother Nature is changing
Everything about is rearranging
The old is changed into the new
Fullmoon drops mix with the dew.
Souls are deep in meditation
Minds are set on the path of liberation
Visions of Self and Life as the whole
Learning the keys to the energies of the Soul

FOR NOTES
Insights, Reflections, Self-Observations

FOR NOTES
Insights, Reflections, Self-Observations

CHAPTER 9:
The Soul as Sacred Mandala

The soul of Mother Africa is a sacred mandala—the Circle Unbroken. The Mandala as a primal symbol of "Mother Africa Within" serves as the Magic Circle of the Self and is seen as the Circle which has its Center everywhere and its circumference nowhere. "Mother Africa within" serves as the Center of the Soul because She is the primal "Source of Creation." Therefore, a variety of techniques and approaches are used to help facilitate the initiation or rites-of-passage into the Center.

Recognition of the Center
Identification with the Center
Internalization of the Center
Absorption in the Center
Expansion of the Center

Expansion of the Center Since the Mandala is undefinable and unknowable in rational terms we can gain access to it only by way of description and participation.

Descriptions of Qualities and Traits of the Mandala

The simplest description of the Mandala is that it is symbolized as a circle – rotating wheel – of energy. Mandala is the Wheel of the Soul, the Wheel of Consciousness, the Wheel of the Whole.

It is the Wheel of Health and Well-being.

> The Mandala is the Wheel of Attunement to the cosmic laws of the Unified field of Energy/The Beloved Community.

> It is the Wheel of initiation from the state of dis-ease to the state of Ease.

The Mandala is the "wheels within a wheel". It is the wheel of consciousness of the soul-character-ego-personality-SOUL as it seeks reunion with the SELF/SOUL. It is the Wheel of Maturation/Initiation from the unknowing, untrained state to the All-Knowing, Trained State of SELF Consciousness.

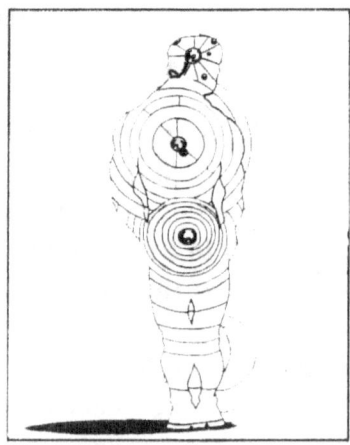

Mandala of Inner Space

Each level of our being, or each charkra level contains a major mandala which serves as the organizing center of associated groups of submandalas.

The Law of Center and Centering

The Law of Center is central to the Mandala. The Mandala is known as the circle which has its center everywhere and its circumference nowhere. At the center of the Mandala resides the organizing nucleus of the Soul as the Hidden Indweller. This indwelling organizing nucleus of divinity has been variously spoken of throughout various cultures at Nut, Horus, Christ, Ori, Oro, Buddha, Isis, Hathor and other names.

The inner Symbolic/Energy Complex Systems and the soul-personality-ego- character-SOUL are constantly taking us through experiences to help us develop our sense of "Oneness" and wholeness of the "SELF" (the soul spelled in small letters refer to the material soul and when spelled in large letters refers to the spiritual Soul—the Higher Self). When any one part of the Self gets too far out of balance, there is a call, a pull from the deep inner Center for the return into the balanced state of wholeness with the Heart, our natural-spiritual Self—Mother Africa Within.

The inner natural-spiritual Self is known to us culturally through the various traditional rituals to the ancestors and through the various processes of inner knowing such as intuition, dreams, revelations and creative vision.

It is fitting and proper that we begin our journey into the process of maturation by paying proper respect to this inner realm of the ancestors. The ancestors are the symbols of that which is highest and deepest within us, and most deserving of respect. These inner symbols of Self belong to the realm of intuition and the right brain. The right brain is the seat of memories, the seat of the Soul and the Unconscious Mind. The right-brain is the old brain and its functions constitute the "original," "earlier" or the "primitive" way of knowing reality. This "primitive" designation has caused the right brain, which has its early evolutionary development in African and Eastern matriarchal cultures, to be thought of as evil and negative.

Africa has historically been labelled the "Dark Continent" less because of the color of the skin of its inhabitants, but more because of its association with the rituals and communion with ancestral, natural and spiritual forces. The mystique of the African past has been passed down through the generations and today creates an aura of mysticism of the Ameri-Africentric soul-personality-ego-character-SOUL that formulates the Soulful Worldview held by the African-American, African-Caribbean and all African people outside of Africa. The Ameri-Africentric soul-personality-ego-character-SOUL herein refers to all the people of the Americas, North, South, Central and Caribbean islands who have lineage, claimed or unclaimed, pure or mixed, in the African tradition.

The African Aspect of the Ameri-Africentric soul-personality-ego-Character-SOUL has its roots in the right brain or intuitive-spiritual culture of Africa that evolves around the central principles of:

1. Vital Force," "Force-Vitale, "Soul Force", ntu-force
2. Ancestral communication and the continuity of the Soul
3. Rhythm with its ability to awaken Soul energy, integrate and harmonize the individual with the collective community.
4. Transcendence
5. Karma

Centering is the central evolutionary process of the Vital Force or Soul Force. This centering function of Soul Force synthesizes all of the lessons and experiences of the previous stages of growth into a coherent whole. At each level of maturation, this integrated whole can be transcended on the way to a higher and more expansive expression and realization of the Self. As such, centering involves a consolidation of energies and forces, a dying and rebirth of transcendence –like the catapillar which withdraws into a cocoon to undergo the secret, mystical transformation only later to emerge as the beautiful butterfly.

The Metamorphosis

The process of Centering is closely allied and interwoven with the concept of internalization of symbols of Self-Mastery, Self-Empowerment, Self-Representation, Self-Control, Self-Realization and symbols of Spiritual Cultural I-dentification.

The process of Centering turns one's symbolic energies back upon the inner depths of the Soul and Self to find inner meaning and the proper context of relations to the Self, Family, Community and Society. This proper context of relations will define self-expression that assures harmonious development, submission to, and union with, the Self in the family, the culture, the society, the nation and Self Within—all being but different aspects of One I-dentity and One Reality—the I-dentity which empowers and transcends circumstance and time.

Centering generates a transcendental, refined energy from the innerself—a force capable of bringing about great healing and creative changes—a Soul Force of "Ache". Ache in the Yoruba tradition of West Africa is simplistically defined as the spiritual power to make things happen. Ultimately, at the center of all transcendental Centering processes, is the introduction into, and integration with the icons of the timeless, changeless, eternal realms of law and energy that govern the Soul, Nature, Universe and the Inner "kingdom Of

Oneness". This inner changeless realm has already been referred to in this book as the "Growing Ancestral World Tree".

Growing Ancestral World Tree

Through the Centering process, the child is taught not "what" to learn but "how" to learn, how to "listen to" and tap the deep sources of knowledge and healing from within for purposes of growth, creativity and maturation. Centering therefore provides one with new inner organizational skills of viewing the family, community and the world and one's place in, and relationship to the family, community and the world. Centering provides new patterns and strengths for intervening in the world, for Co-Participating in the process of Creation and Re-Creation.

Centering puts one in touch with those universal inner symbol-energy systems, themes, patterns of behavior that serve as the motivation and foundation of conscious behavior.

In the absence of a planned and controlled symbolic initiation into the forces and energies of the Soul—a spontaneous, natural initiation occurs at the intuitive level and without proper guidance, often becomes deviant and destructive, i.e.—centering into street gangs, drug societies and demonic cults.

Centering is essentially a continuous experience at both the individual and the collective level and points in the direction of new healing energies for the future as the world collectively enters into a new scientific-spiritual era-- the era of the Science of the Soul. This is the era of the Spiritual—Rational Being, the era of the balanced "Community of Oneness".

Things that Prevent Us from Centering

Blocks to centering are blocks to the internalization of symbols of growth and Self-Maturity. Some of the blocks are:

1. Associations (visual, emotional, sentimental)
2. Anxiety
3. Fear
4. Attachment to material things and/or persons
5. Drugs, i.e. marijuana, alcohol, crack, etc.
6. Worry
7. Doubt
8. Hate
9. Anger
10. Prejudices
11. Emotions
12. Lack of concentration
13. Insincerity
14. Lying
15. Cheating
16. Stealing
17. Wrong diet
18. Wrong use of sexual energy
19. A major concentration of energies on planning and working toward things in the future, rather than closing off things in the present.

Correct centering relationships can only take place in the NOW. Proper transactions with the Center of Heart of Soul allow the NOW to become ever present and expansive. One may be sorry and remorseful and repent after something wrong is done, but the NOW has passed and he/she can only hope to correct him/herself in the next presentation of that situation in one of its variety of forms in the future. The corrected response to that situation must be brought into the present through "presentification" (making real in the present according to universal spiritual Laws of the Soul) or "SASA-fication" (Sasa is an african word for the same concept of the spiritualized **present** moment).

Some of the Centering Techniques are:

1. Individual, family and group counseling employing both traditional western psychological techniques and theories as well as African-Eastern theories, techniques and practices.
2. Yoga and integrative disciplines such as Tae Kwon Do, Tai Chi—which are martial arts forms built on the central unifying principle of Chi or Soul Force Energy.
3. Arts and Crafts designed to awaken and vitalize the symbol-making functions of the innerself (Soul) and put them in the service of understanding and improving attitudes-values-behaviors.
4. Soul (Ori) centered Meditation, Visualization and Inner Transformation Workshops – designed to identify and rename blocks in the different energy fields of the Soul in order that the soul-personality-character can be more fully seated in its True Center of I-dentity—the SOUL or SELF.

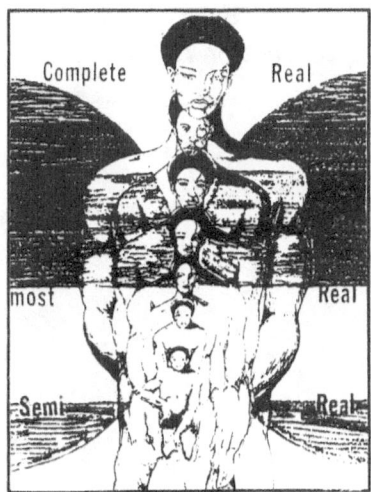

Centering in the Self

5. Mandala Self-Healing Circles – community self-help group approaches to surfacing the symbols of inner soul-personality-character-SOUL development.
6. Parenting, Extended-Family and Community Awareness Groups-Parent training and consciousness raising workshops focused on examining and correcting the influence of cultural Life – Track and life-style issues on soul-personality-ego-character-SOUL development.
7. Mandala Pilgrimage Travel Tours – Tours in quest of cultural-symbolic-spiritual enlightenment to major spiritual power-sites of Africa, Asia, India, South America and Caribbean Islands.

FOR NOTES
Insights, Reflections, Self-Observations

CHAPTER 10:
The Soul-centered Model

The Soul-centered Healing model is a model that integrates the all important and central element of the SOUL as the core of the learning, knowing, growth, maturation and Self-Realization processes.

It is a model that starts with the child as symbol of the soul-personality-ego-character-SOUL at the beginning of the process at the physical level and ends with the Child-Like state of Innocent Love and Truth at the end of the process on the Spiritual Level. The beginning and the end are one and the same, and are caught up in each other as the cyclical, self-renewing process of the Circle Unbroken or Mandala of Life. This Self-renewing, unbroken circle of the soul-personality-ego-character-SOUL in ancient tradition was symbolized as the uroborous—or the serpent which swallows its tail.

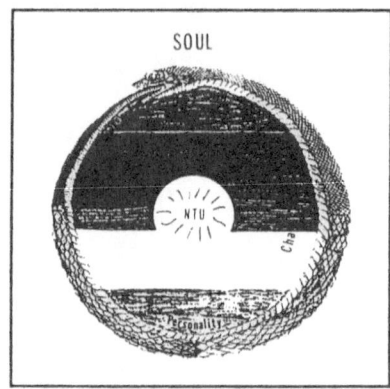

Uroborous

The Uroborous

The child is the nuclear symbol from, and to, which the family, community and society evolves in an ever re-occurring cyclical process of development, maturation and individuation. The highest symbol of the perfect society, the Kingdom, the Beloved Community, the Promised Land starts in, and can only be entered in the Child-Like state.

The soul-personality-ego-character-SOUL matures through childhood, adolescence, adulthood, maturity and the development of later child-like simplicity represented in the state of "One Community Consciousness". This involves a series of progressive inner stage-related movements in growth, maturation, consolidation of I-dentity, and unfoldment of the soul-personality-ego-character-SOUL. This is a holistic development and involves not only the child level but the family, community, world and cosmic levels.

The one central part of the person that remains constant, yet expands and grows through all of the stages is the central nucleus of Self—(Ori), Nut, Isis, Horus, Christ—the Divine Innerself—the Indweller—the Light. In optimal development, one stage is gradually given up and incorporated into the next higher level as one undertakes the Mystic Transformation and growth on the new level. Each new stage that one enters upon is but an introduction into another aspect of the Self. Initiation then, in its simplest definition means "an introduction into". What one should be progressively

116

"introduced into" are the higher states or spheres of functioning in the Material-Rational-Spiritual Society and Cosmos. Ultimately, one is introduced into the Spiritual-Transcendental aspects of the Self that constitute the higher states of consciousness and the "Community of Oneness"—The "Beloved Community". This means a collective sharing and management of the means and resources of empowerment and enrichment of culture for the upliftment of humanity.

Each of these stages from childhood to the perfect internally-integrated pluralistic societal model of the "One Transcendental Community" has its characteristics. These stage-related characteristics include behaviors, drives, emotions, sentiments, values, morals, beliefs, interests, desires, and manifestations.

The growing person from childhood through the various stages of maturation is forever changing, getting rid of old, as well as incorporating new-feelings, values, interest, desires of more advanced stages.

In her search, the person releases the behaviors of the stages she has left behind only to find that those behaviors re-appear in the interior of her soul-personality-ego-character-SOUL at a new and higher order of meaning. However, in Black children, because of the many and varied oppressive variables hindering their development, this frequently does not occur in the normal stages or at normal times demanded by growth, survival and maturity.

The Levels of the Mandala of the soul-personality-ego-character-SOUL

There are eleven major levels of the Mandala Soul-Centered Model. They make up the Mandala of the Self which constitutes the various Soul Forces or Imago-Symbolic-Energy-Complex Systems. Each level generates and requires a different consciousness of health and growth rules.

In the below diagram the word "plexus" refers to the collection of parasympathetic nerves gathered as nodes throughout various parts of the body, which govern autonomic, cyclical functions of the body, personality-ego-character and Soul. In East Indian culture, these nodes are referred to as Charkas.

These eleven levels intersphere with each other as two interlocking triangles—one pointed upward and the other pointed downward. In ancient alchemical tradition, this concept was demonstrated as the two Trees in the Garden—the Tree of Knowledge of Good and Evil and the Tree of Life.

Trees in the Garden

Level VII Self, Christ, Buddha, Isis (pineal Plexus)

Level VI Hero(ine) Ipituitary Plexus)

Level V Ancestral World Tree (thyroid Plexus)

Level IV Love (heart) (thymus Plexus)

Level III Paternal/male/masculine/will Power (celiac Plexus)

Level II Maternal/female/feminine/nurturance (genital Plexus)

Level I Child/trickster/path finder/fool (caudal Plexus)

Level II The Indwelling Light

Level III The "ground Of Being"/the Unknown/the Interphase/the Womb Of The Dark Mother

Level XI The Integrator—the soul-personality-ego-character-SOUL

These imago-template levels constitute the various levels of Consciousness. Consciousness is Divine Power, (Ache). Divine Power or Ache gives one the ability to "Make things happen." Divine Power or Ache is consciousness.

By developing consciousness of ourselves, of the blindspots, as well as the strengths in our interactions as we transgress the various imago-metaphoric fields of consciousness (neters), we heal ourselves. This process is called working on the inner planes.

FOR NOTES
Insights, Reflections, Self-Observations

CHAPTER 11:

Soul Force
The Manifestations of Soul Force—Ache
(Faculties of the Self)

The Wisdom of the Soul and its Powers

Throughout the oral and written traditions of Africa, India, Meso-America (Aztec, Cuban, Haitian, Mayans) south America (Lucumi, Condomble), there is mention of unusual powers of the Soul. These unusual powers have included the power of levitation, transformation, power to diagnose and heal, power to harm and kill, transportation, astral travel, precognition, telepathy and others. "Ache" is a Yoruba word from West Africa used to describe the powers of the Soul that "make things happen" beyond what the logical mind can understand. Ache brings things into being, as if from nowhere.

These powers are employed by those who have a certain knowledge of Soul culture and its wisdom. People who have these powers have built up a certain amount of Ache (spiritual-psychic power) through their successive life cycles and proper relationship to, and respect for, the Soul Forces. We create and evolve the world through Ache—the power to make things happen.

Regardless of time or culture, the hidden and invisible Soul Forces or M.I.S.E.S.C. speak to similar, universal realities and point in similar directions, some of which are:

1. There are three qualitatively different aspects of the mind inhabiting the human psyche or Soul. These are the intuitive-imaginal, the rational-logical and the Spiritual-Rational-Intuitive. The latter is a synthetic mode which is a higher mode than the imaginal or rational and occupies the interphase between the two.

2. There is another, more important, and far vaster aspect of the Self than that which we know as the material, visible reality and ego. The material, visible reality is but a limited expression in a continuous cycle of evolving, spiritualizing conscsiousness.

3. There are invisible, intelligent forces and complexes of the spirit world that shape the manifestations of the natural and the material world. These invisible, intelligent forces use us as vehicles of their symbolization and expression.

4. Life is continuous and we experience that continuity through the M.I.S.E.S.C. and the symbolizations of the Soul or Innerself.

5. There are spiritual powers and healing potentials in the Soul or Innerself that supercede intellect and reasoning. i.e. – these healing energies are witnessed in such phenomena as laying on of hands and various other miraculous healings.

6. The Soul develops concomitantly, and parallel, to the "mind" and body. The growth of the Soul requires the same amount, if not more, attention, dedication, discipline and devotion in its development as the rational mind, physical body and emotions.

The M.I.S.E.S.C. or Soul Forces form an underlying universal language of "mother-wit" which has existed since the dawn of evolution. These Soul Forces continue today to serve as the matrix for the apperception and perception of reality. Apperception is the mode of cognition of the right-brain—i.e. intuition, revelations, spiritual experiences. Perception is the mode of cognition of the left-brain—i.e. logical, concrete, material experiences.

The inner "secret" process of the integrative workings of the M.I.S.E.S.C. or Soul Forces has been the object of study of "secret societies" since before the beginnings of recorded history. The study of the Soul Forces perhaps has its first manifestations in recorded history in the hieroglyphics of ancient Egypt. In more modern times, this secret process continues to be the object of study in psychology, religion, sociology, anthropology and even modern physics.

Soul Forces are cosmic forces that inhabit the universe as well as the "unconscious" mind/Soul. Therefore, we live within the different force fields of the Archetypal/Neter/Orisha/Soul Forces as well as they live within us as character traits, desires, instincts, drives and habit patterns. They swell through the deep tunnels of the unconscious mind and perpetually reinforce symbols in the conscious everyday life as motivated attitudes, values and behaviors. They constitute both the "Shadow" and the "Spirit of Enlightenment" in human behavior. The Positive Shadow and the Spirit of Enlightment collectively constitute the Mandala Rising.

As the Mandala rises and we are put in touch with the "Wisdom of the Soul", we gain the ability to know and handle these Soul Forces as inner psychic powers. These powers reside within each of us as faculties (indwelling properties) of the Soul, we have but to develop and use them. Emanation (vibes) of "Fluids" of Ache come from major areas of the Body and Soul.

Third Eye
Eyes
Hands
Charkras
Non-Verbal Language
Mind
Voice, Throat
Heart
Solar Plexus (Umbilicus)
Genitals

Emanations are constantly being given off and picked up as ("Vibes")

1. One's Soul Force grows and can be perceived or known by others in proportion to the amount of Love and/or Truth that one lives. This is also spoken of as Integrity and/or Presence.
2. Soul Force (Ache) is Essence and is based on the Law of Cause and Effect. Nothing comes into existence without a cause.

In the religious-political contexts that cultures usually assume, Life-Style themes, issues and symbols and the desires they create depend upon "competitive value assignment". This competitive value assignment is based on in-group, cultural and racial membership, socio-economic class, sexual role preference and Life-style. Themes which transcend these membership differences belong to the Life-Track and are absolute, universal, transcultural and transpersonal in nature. It is this Life-Track group of symbolic themes that I have already referred to as Mandala-Imago-Symbolic-Energy-System Complexes (M.I.S.E.S.C.) or "Soul Forces". They would in a comparable way, in their deeper aspects, be synonymous with the Archetypes, Orishas and Neters. They comprise an ever evolving axis of electro-magnetic energy which will be referred to periodically as the Growing Ancestral World Tree or just as the Ancestral World Tree.

A complex of "Soul Forces" would be, at some levels, similar to the "archetypes" of Carl Jung and exist on many different determinative levels at one time with many different attributes such as specific colors, plants, stones, jewels, animals, songs, musical notes, days, foods, and other correlations through the various realms of nature. These Soul Forces serve as the bridges between the human and non-human worlds and between the invisible and the visible worlds.

These "Natural Soul Forces" are organizing forces of the Innerself (unconscious mind) which lead to concepts, ideas, values and behaviors being organized into some coherent context in conscious behavior. This latter process could be referred to as "contextualization". These Soul

Forces allow the participant to undergo the "mystic transformation" from instinctual human to Divine Human. This transformation from the human to the Divine constitutes the "African Science" which is the accumulated knowledge in the collective consciousness of a people of how to live in tune with the non-human world of Mother Nature and the invisible spiritual world of God. The Orishal Soul Forces collectively constitute the feminine principle or "Mother Nature" forces. The Soul Forces are the different aspects of the natural and non-human world which constitute the unconscious, historical and social mind both at the personal and the collective level. Each Orishal Soul Force is but another interpretation or representation of the One Great Reality.

The Western world, even though unwittingly participating in these Soul Forces, has denied their existence and has repressed them as dark, evil, instinctual, feminine and negative. This repression came about primarily because of their African and feminine origins and connotations. The "Soul Forces" got repressed in western psychology under the mask of the "Id". Freud took the concept of the Id from his colleague's, Greog Groddeck's book, The It (Das Ich). In Groddeck's work, the It had the connotation of a high healing Spiritual Energy of Mother Nature.

The scientific world, as well as the rest of the world, awaits the re-integration of these Soul Forces as vital aspects of psychic life in order to restore equilibrium and balance to the rational mind. The re-integration of the Soul Forces would constitute a return to the Source—the Heart of Soul. The birth of that which is highest in humanity always comes from a return, an acknowledgement of the Primal Paradise—the Origins—Mother—Source—The beginnings—Mother Africa Within. These Soul Forces or (M.I.S.E.S.C.) are autonomous complexes of the unconscious mind. As the imago-symbolic-complexes become more perfected and autonomous, they are primarily housed in that region of the unconscious mind/Soul which Freud labelled as the "Systematic Unconscious" and which is called the Zamani in certain parts of Africa. The Soul Forces have their influences and manifestations in the everyday habit traits of the various "life-styles". These imago-symbolic-complexes or Soul Forces manifest in attitudinal-value-behavioral expressions in our daily interactions and exchanges. Therefore, they are constantly in evolution—moving from the concrete experiences of everyday life into the fixed patterns of universal experiences and visa-versa. These imago-symbolic-complexes or Soul Forces form a feedback, circular-spiraling system that has been, and will be, unbroken throughout time. This continuous feedback system is commonly referred to in Africentric culture as "the Circle Unbroken"—which is the uroborous.

In describing the aesthetic, ethical and creative expressions of African people, one first thinks about the concept of holism. From this whole perception of life and reality, there is no separation among these various categories. They blend in the modalities of utility and functionalism which are central to the african "symbol-producing process", whether in music, dance, poetry, statues, masks, etc. The arts and creative expressions exist to serve developmental needs of the individual, only in relation to the group and the ancestral/spiritual world of God. Therefore, in traditional African society, these creative expressions of Soul Force were produced in such a way as to appease and call upon the forces of the spiritual and natural worlds, both for protection and for vitalizing the functions of the community. They allowed human participation in the unseen mysterious forces of life.

Generative Theme Trigger Questions for Group/family/One-to-one Interactions

How is Soul Force related to Essence?
How is Soul Force related to Magnetism?
How is Soul Force related to Presence?
How is Soul Force related to Love?
How is Soul Force related to Truth?
How is Soul Force related to Life?
How is Soul Force related to the Theory of Relativity?
How is Soul Force related to One's vibes?
How does one generate Soul Force?
How is Soul Force related to Self-Realization?

Appendix

A.

1. Soul Force is a way of being in _____
   _____

2. Soul Force is a way of seeing _____
   _____

3. Soul Force is a way of awakening to _____
   _____

4. Sour Force is a way of relating to _____
   _____

5. Soul Force is a way of understanding _____
   _____

6. Soul Force is a way of practicing _____
   _____

7. Soul Force is a way of living _____
   _____

8. Soul Force is a way of dying to _____
   _____

9. Soul Force is a way of being reborn in _____
   _____

B.

10. Soul Force is my _____
    _____

11. Soul Force helps me to _____
    _____

12. Soul Force can _____
    _____

13. Soul Force will _____
    _____

14. Soul Force has _____
    _____

C. Write a paragraph on Martin Luther King's and Mahatma Gandhi's philosophy of Soul Force.

Soul Forcers

(Seekers and practitioners of the Soul-Centered approaches)

1. Builders in an evolving society, (the Beloved Community) of Righteous Behavior and "Living Patterns". This Righteous Society will allow for the full Self-Realization of human spiritual potentials. The Beloved Community is a pluralistic society in which harmony, balance, peace, rhythm, love and respect are "lived" phenomena as envisioned by Martin Luther Kind, Jr.
2. Conscious participants in a total living and life space experience with Self, Community and Nature, employing behavioral-attitudinal-value orientations and spiritual techniques for growth and maturation.
3. Conscious participants in utilizing the corrective modes of Soul-Centered, Spiritual-Humanistic living and thinking about Self and other in everyday life.
4. Conscious participants in building bridges of respect, truth, trust, dignity, understanding, patience, confidence, better communication in establishing the Beloved Community of Oneness.
5. Conscious participants in working to unfold those highest creative potentials in the soul-personality-ego-character which will lead to Self-Realization and union with the higher SOUL.
6. Conscious participants in a Soul-Centered extended family; developmental-support group concept which views the family—extended family and community as being the primary agent in the healing/growth process.

Internalization of Symbols of Self Control, Soul Force and Ache

Using the philosophy of Soul Force as a background for the discussion, have the students answer and associate to the following symbolic areas of soul-personality-ego-character-SOUL growth.

I.   Responsibility

1. Definitions: Give a word definition or symbol association and example of the two word phrases:

   a. cultural responsibility
   b. cultural obligation

2. Trigger Questions:

   a. How are cultural responsibility and obligations associated with or related to "right actions?"
   b. How are cultural responsibility and obligations associated with Righteousness and Community?
   c. Define your cultural responsibility to your family, friends, self, extended family, school, community.
   d. What cultural obligations do you have to your family, friends, self, extended family, school, community?
   e. How do you feel you carry out your cultural responsibility and obligations in the above listed areas.
   f. Do you feel that you have too many or too little cultural obligations and responsibilities.
   g. If you could get rid of some of your cultural obligations and responsibilities, which ones would they be?
   h. Do you ever take on extra cultural responsibilities without being asked or forced?
   i. If you could take on extra cultural responsibilities, which would you like to take on?

j. How do you think the following persons would assess your sense of cultural responsibility?—parents, brothers, sisters, friends and teachers.

k. Where do cultural obligations and responsibilities come from?

l. Before your parents were born, where did cultural obligations and responsibilities come from?

m. Why is it important to have cultural responsibilities and obligations?

3. Attitudinal-Value-Behavioral Assignments

a. Learn to spell the word phrases "cultural obligation" and "cultural responsibility".

b. Find a way to express your very own feelings about these two words either through a poem, a paragraph, a picture collage, or a drawing.

c. Meditate/visualize on both an area of weakness and an area of strength in your Soul Force of Obligation and Responsibility.

d. Become aware of the "ripple-effect" in the area of increasing patterns of Obligation and Responsibility and record them in a diary/journal.

e. Construct and direct a video cassette of this trait either through interview, role playing or any combination of techniques.

FOR NOTES
Insights, Reflections, Self-Observations

FOR NOTES
Insights, Reflections, Self-Observations

CHAPTER 12:

Internalization of the Symbols of
Self-Mastery and Self-Transcendence

The process of I-dentification and maturation has to be viewed and approached in the correct context as a transcendental synthesis and a centering process. This centering process results in the internalization of symbols of Self-Control, Self-Mastery and Self-Transcendence. Each successive stage of I-dentification is one of transcendence wherein the past stage is not perceived because it has been internalized and the person shalt have become that stage him/herself. This demonstrates the value of letting go of attachment to material symbols exclusively. This is the process of "incorporation of the umwelt (worldview)" and would involve putting the mastery of outer experience inside of one's Self. As this process of incorporation increases, the lower self is negated and the Higher Soul or Self is freed from matter, enhanced and its boundaries are extended, its wisdom deepened and its power increased, the goal (symbol) disappears, because one has become that symbol, only to reappear at a higher level of symbolism, forever drawing the Soul-Seeker towards Truth and a deeper understanding, expression and Unfoldment of the Self.

Each successive stage that is incorporated and transcended becomes a part of the soul-personality-ego-character-SOUL as the "I". The "I" is the center of Self definition which gives the person a sense of "Beingness", belonging, continuity, I-dentity, purpose and direction. This internal synthesis and integration leads to the "Mission" of achieving a sense of Oneness. As this feeling of "I" increases, so does the Inner Light of Self Knowledge. The person is able to let his/her Light so shine that others may see his/her good works.

As this process increases, the Christ Spirit of Love, the Buddha Spirit of Compassion and the Spirits of Faith, Hope, Truth and Light unfold their energies. This unfoldment occurs through the synthesis, integration, centering and transcendental processes of the soul-personality-ego-character on its relentless Journey Into Self and search for Re-Union with the Heart of SOUL, the Source—Mother Africa Within.

The role of cultural myth, ritual and initiation is to facilitate this process of Symbolization, growth and transformation of the Soul Forces. Myth, ritual and initiation, especially facilitate the Central Coordinating Nucleus of Self through the stages of internalization into Self-Mastery and Transcendence. Utilizing the tools of myth and ritual allows repressed, dormant and quiescent images and symbols to emerge and take on substance through facilitating their entry into the conscious (aware/rational) mind and their subsequent expansion and extension in time, space and eternity. For example:

A. The hair rituals of the Black Power movement during the 1960's. Originally there were attempts to tie these rituals to their deeper symbolic/archetypal roots—those symbols rooted in the collective cultural pool. Hair in Black culture is significantly related to power and roots.

B. Widely held covert belief systems of the Africentric community both on the continent and in the diaspora, about death and the survival of the Soul in the ancestral spirit world are allowed to come into conscious awareness through childrearing practices, religious practices, symbolic-manipulation and discussion. This also involves their subsequent expansion.

The goal of using ritual, and initiation is to increase:

1. The "participation mystique" or in other words, to motivate larger and larger numbers of the people in the community to participate in the search for the higher, more positive levels of consciousness.
2. Initiation is an age old mechanism of soul-mind-energy dynamics established to convert personal individualistic energy through the instillation of feelings of Community relatedness and the internalization of that Community's system of ethics and values.

The necessary transition and transcendence of the current situation which involves a predominantly left-brain oriented "rationally", thinking society, to a more balanced usage of our total power (mind, soul, body) cannot and should not occur overnight or hastily. This transition requires an infinite amount of planning, action, repetition, sacrifice, commitment, growth, transformation, maturation and development. It is a step by step progression involving many levels of development. It involves a process of "Return to the Source", a reversion to some of the earlier modes of behavior which would be considered "root behaviors" in the cultural axis of a people. These root behaviors would be those behaviors which have allowed them to surmount, overcome and transcend the many hurdles to their development in the past. In this sense, the return of the roots or Source could be considered a turning-point, a counter-movement or a crisis. Of course, this has to be balanced at all times with necessary force in the opposite direction (left-brain) to create the necessary psychological tension to energize acts of transcendence of moving to a higher level of awareness.

Psychological tension can be generated by graduated expectations, in a holistic manner, integrating rational—intellectual, as well as, and most importantly, intuitive—contemplative faculties. The best mode of such graduated expectations is through the ancient ritual of initiation and "Rites of Passage" which involves an "introduction to new" expectations and "closure of old" methods of behavior. This transition partakes of the laws of: Cause and Effect, seriality and finality.

Conservation of Energy

1. Closure—events, debts, personal obligations, promises, projects, assignments should be closed off or brought to a point of summation to serve as foundation and starting point for new activities otherwise drainage occurs through open energy channels.
2. Symbolic and ritual incorporation and closure is necessary to produce psychological tension, direction and transcendence. This process was facilitated in ancient Nature-Centered cultures through the participation of the Council of Elders. Conscience and constructive guilt are the major ingredients as well as outcome of the closure-transcendence situation. It is the "presence" of Truth that generates life because it is a "streaming" and is life; this "presence" generates conscience and transcendence.

Transcendence involves a synthesis, a closure, a bringing together of disparate parts to make a whole (I-dentification); it is a healing phenomenon. After synthesis, centering, I-dentification and transcendence of the acts and incorporation of the symbols has occurred, the lower senses that cognize (know) those symbols can be transcended and the symbols later released so that one's attachment to them become a thing of the past.

As the mind/Soul synthesizes these symbols, senses and experiences and makes them a thing of the past, a state of spiritual and transcendental reason, knowing and Being is established. Transcendental Reason, Spiritual-Rational Reason is also described as Buddha, Christ, Isis, and other perfected divine states of consciousness.

Transcendental Reason is a "Whole" state of cognition and consciousness. It improves logical reason which is of the intellect and has been kept apart from the intuitive mind whose nature is love—wisdom. Transcendental Reason is the Christ—life or principle, which in the process of taking incarnation or form, as we know it, manifests forth as the specific and the unspecific.

Transcendental reasoning combines:

A. perceptual, intellectual lower rational—logic and scientific method.
B. Intuitive—Spiritual-Contemplative reason, higher rational-pure reason.

Transcendental Reasoning or Higher Spiritual-Rational Intuition is a higher form of mind than the intuitive and/or the rational. It occupies the interphase between the two. It could best be thought of as Ma-atified reality which integrates both the intuitive and the logical as they are synthesized through Right-Choice, Right-Action and Truth.

It is only by coming in touch with the Life Force ourselves through Right Choice and Right-Action and attempting to help other do the same can we hope to move our society to a level of awareness where we can avail ourselves of the healing forces of Universal Life and achieve global health and Peace. We must all seek to teach and learn. Holistic Soul-Centered learning can only proceed from Presence. The teacher can only give Presence and attempt to teach others their paths if he/she has internalized and incorporated the moral principles of Universal Law and is living Truth. Students have to perceive the Presence of their teacher, children have to perceive the Presence of their parents and visa versa. It is the Presence which generates force. Presence is "livingness" and occurs only after the symbol has been internalized, incorporated, integrated and is either on its way to being, or has been, released or transcended. Presence is a state of being totally committed.

In helping children to find their paths, the most important things to remember are:

1. That this approach cannot be "taught" per se, but rather must be "lived". The teacher must join the student in a process of discovery and unfoldment.

2. Many children are further along in their development on the path of transition than the teacher may be, so it will be important for the teacher to act as a catalyst of invocation and provocation as well as becoming a student while the student becomes the teacher.

3. The overriding goal at all times is to establish synergy and transcendence, so that sacrifice, commitment and dedication is involved at all levels. The one rule to serve as a guiding light is the Golden Rule—Do Unto Others, As You Would Have Them Do Unto You. The transition cannot be sought with personal desires and selfish motivations otherwise one loses the path and falls into confusion and regressive behavioral patterns. Regressive behavioral and attitudinal traits impede the act of Transcendence.

4. The movement or "path of transition" into the center is a movement into Oneness, a movement into the Supreme I-dentity, a discovery of the "Self" or the "I AM" that is within. This I-dentification, growth, maturation and transcendence are all field phenomena. They involve various interactions between the child and his/her environment. Some of these interactions are more important to the formative sense of self-concept and I-dentity than others. Also some stages and ages are more important than others in forming the sense of Self and I-dentity.

FOR NOTES
Insights, Reflections, Self-Observations

FOR NOTES
Insights, Reflections, Self-Observations

CHAPTER 13:

Laws Of The Soul

Laws Of The Inner Self

The soul-personality-ego-character-SOUL is governed, controlled and directed in its development and maturation by Laws of the Innerself.

One's journey into the realm of the Soul and into the Higher Realm of the Self is guided and controlled by the universal built-in spiritual – natural Laws. There are myriad paths leading to the one goal of Self – Realization. These inner Laws assure that each seeker reaches the goal.

The Laws govern the energies of the Soul. Brunton in his book "The Spiritual Crisis of Man" states: "The cosmic laws exist, for if they did not, everything would be in confusion." These Laws of the Soul regulate the smooth operation of all that is in nature and the cosmos. They assure that one season will follow another in an orderly progression. They assure that the mother's milk will be ready for the baby after birth. They assure that the sun will rise each morning and set each evening. They assure that the fruit will be bourne on the tree of its kind. These Laws provide the context of human free will and morality. These Laws provide humans with a choice, even if in the end the choice is no choice. For the ultimate choice is the submission of free will to the harmony of the Laws of Mother Nature as expressive of the WILL of GOD.

These Laws guide the development of the soul-personality-ego-character-SOUL of the individual-family-community and nation. The development of the soul-personality-ego-character-SOUL takes place in accordance, and collaboration, with conscious choice and will to change and grow. It might also be said that these inner Laws of the SOUL guide the process of conscious choice.

C.D.A.C--T.D.P.D Diagram

All of the Laws of the Soul, like the various levels of imago-symbolic-templates, in some respect reflect and mirror each other. They all express the Divine Indwelling aspect of God in the soul-personality-ego-character-SOUL of the cosmos as well as in the individual and group.

The Law of God and Soul is enforced, executed and administered by the deities, gods, orishas, neters, loas, archetypes, ancestors, as well as other natural forces and spirits. The Law of God and the Soul is the orderly working out of the principle of Being or the Divine Ideal into Expression and Manifestation throughout Creation.

The Laws of the Soul ensure a harmonious integration of the higher values of the SOUL with the lower values of the soul so that a creative synthesis is achieved. Through choice, decision and action, we create and symbolize at various levels of the Soul's energy field. The Soul is the realm in and through which the Higher and lower realms of Law operate.

Law of Karma (Cause and Effect)

Gaskell states:

> "Karma is the law of causation and interaction between the higher and lower planes to bring about equilibrium between them and gradually raise the Soul."

Karma synthesizes and integrates the Higher Soul with the lower soul, the masculine with the feminine, the good with the bad. It is through Karma that the many experiences of former lives are utilized to bring the soul-personality-ego-character unto union with the higher SELF, the SOUL and with COMMUNITY—THE BALANCED STATE OF MA-AT.

The Law of Cause and Effect is designed in such a manner that each individual/group encounters those trials or experiences that are most needed in the growth and maturational experience. These experiences are generated from two levels, those we have control over through our daily choices and use/misuse of will power, and those we have no control over and which are determined from the Higher Mind.

Heaney in his book—The Sacred and The Psychic, states "A major Christian theological objection to the doctrine of 'Karma' is the Law of Cause and Effect." He gives a strong case that in Christian theology, **faith, forgiveness** and **grace** are the x-factors that even alters Karma so that there is not always a direct cause and effect relationship in our development and union with God and the higher states of consciousness. He stated that the concept of Karma which includes these factors is very compatible with the doctrine of Christianity.

The objective of the symbolic-associative teaching of this Law of Karma is the development of conscious choice and will. The most important reason for finding symbolic expressions for the Law of Cause and Effect that can be associated to other aspects of the persons life is to help the person realize that they do possess choice and will. Each of us do determine our consequences.

Exercise for Internalizing The Law of Karma

Recontextualization Exercise: Discuss and recontextualize (put into another context) the images from media of the Aggressive Invincible Fighter, the one who tries to jump over and around disaster that he has created—the "evader" of karma—the omnipotent inner child. This imago-template type usually has the feeling that he is able to avoid the head-on collision of contacting the imago of his own undoing.

Dis-Identification Exercise: Visualization of Self-undoing patterns and their consequences and "breaking of the Self-undoing template" in symbolic ways. Mandala exercise and group discussion on dis-identification.

Re-I-dentification Exercise: Master of your fate-Captain of your Soul poem (Invictus), visualization exercise and group mandala exercise.

Contract/Covenant: Establishment of re-channeling goals for the unfreed Soul Force Energy

Law of Correspondence

According to the Dictionary of Symbols, this Law formulates "that cosmic phenomena are limited and serial and that they appear as scales or series on separate planes; but this condition is neither chaotic nor neutral, for the components of one series are linked with those of another in their essence and in their ultimate significance."

The Law of correspondence is related to synesthesia (the meaningful coincidences that can not be explained according to logic). For example when one desperately needs something to happen but there seems to be no logical way that thing could happen and suddenly from some unknown Source the forces are put into play for that thing to happen.

The Law of Correspondence is expressed in the connections between the seven color scales, the scale of temperaments, the seven faculties of the human soul, the seven virtues, seven vices, seven planets, etc.

The Soul operates on a magnetic principle and ripple effect. Any thought and wish you hold steadily in the mind will begin to attract that object or experience to you. This law relates to the fundamental I-dentity and correspondence between things. It can be summarized, "As Above—so below".

All Things are Connected Through a Common I-dentity.

Any thought or image held steady in the mind can be communicated to others over the invisible connecting bridges called Soul "vibes" which are electro-magnetic energy bonds connecting all things, people, animals, time and space.

Training the Invisible Soul Body Exercise

Purpose: To demonstrate the inter-connected of all things through the invisible Soul-Body (Ka Bodies).

Exercise 1: Materials: pencil paper and several decks of E.S.P. cards. The groups should be divided into pairs or groups. Each pair should consist of a sender and the other member(s) of the pair is the receiver. The receiver should be given (30) thirty trial readings with the cards. Depending on the structure of the program, the receivers and sender can exchange positions and the process be repeated.

Exercise 2: Have group concentrate at a given time and hour together each night of the week with one person each night sending and the others receiving.

Exercise 3: During group relaxation-meditation exercise, have everyone concentrate upon "a symbol that unites us all" or some similar theme. They should draw the symbols when they have come out of the meditation and discuss them. The purpose is to look for the similarities and correspondences in the drawings. A further variation on this group exercise would be to have the group form one or more circles and rotate the drawings in the circle so that each person ends up with a drawing different than the one s/he produced. Each person interprets the drawing that s/he has and each person in the circle gets a chance to interpret that drawing also. The person who actually drew that drawing should be the last to interpret the drawing. This process is repeated until all of the drawings have been interpreted.

The group process should be closed with some summation by the facilitator/group leader and a closing ritual of joining hands and later embracing the person to each side or any other appropriate ritual closing for that particular group.

Associative Synthetic Learning
Experience Interconnected of Things

1. Define interconnectedness _____
   _____

2. Write a long paragraph on how this word relates to the invisible Soul-Body _____
   _____

3. What is the relationship between the law of correspondence, interconnectedness and the invisible Soul-Body? _____
   _____

4. List the Seven Levels of the Soul-Centered Model and list one correspondence for each level – be it quality, color, music, plant, animal, symbol, etc. _____

   _____

5. What interconnected experiences can you remember?__

   _____

The Law of Hierarchical Functioning of Imago-templates

The Soul force Symbolic Energy Complexes or imago-templates are arranged in a hierarchial fashion according to their function:

1. Physical
2. Emotional
3. Mental
4. Spiritual

The Law of Manifestation of Energy

Everything comes into being in stages whether it be people, animals, things, ideas, concepts, etc. They exist first in the inner Spiritual World of God and are called forth through the power of Nummo* (word, breath). In coming into being, things pass through at least four general levels:

1. The semi-real world of elemental, spiritual entities and precepts.
2. The almost-real world of concepts and complex energies.
3. In the real-world, closure has occurred. The object has been brought into existence.
4. The Complete Real—pure essence which serves as the back-Ground and the Seed of all levels of the process of manifestation—the Transcended act and object which has now become Essence. The object has been released to be re-grouped at another, higher level of organization.

Exercise

Goal: The teaching of patience, perseverance, follow-through and goal setting.

Everything grows in stages and requires input, energy and nurturance.

Applying The Law to Life

Outline the paths to fulfill the imaginal-Idealized Self.

1. Setting a goal
2. Visualizing the completion of the goal.
3. Mapping out the stages of reaching that Goal.
4. Commitment and follow through.—Allowing the physical to flow into the imaginal-Idealized form. Taking collective responsibility.
5. Sacrifice.

Collective Ritual of Sacrifice – this may include planned periodic fasts, celebration to the ancestors, offerings at the ocean, giving up of bad habits, etc.

Individual rituals of sacrifice – this may include periodic fasts, prayer, meditations and/or visualizations.

Enantiodromia (Reversal Of Opposites)

Law of Enantiodromia: (The Swinging of the pendulum)

This law expresses the inherent tendency of opposites to reverse themselves—the end catches up with the beginning and the beginning is lost in the end.

According to Henderson: "Jung frequently evokes a term used by Heraclitus—enantiodromia, 'running the other way'—to describe a tendency for any myth or 'any psychological or historical and cosmogenic overbalancing' to go over into its opposite."

When attitudes-values and behaviors have become too out of control or one-sided a disaster is often necessary to force the soul-personality-ego-character-SOUL back into a healthy balance.

When you are feeling that you are out of order or headed down a regressive path, are you able to change your course?

The Law of Compensation

It is best described simplistically by Schaer in his book—Religion And The Cure Of The Soul In Jung's Psychology.

"If the conscious mind is unable to correct its one-sideness the compensatory activity of the unconscious begins to function. The unconscious sets about preparing a new attitude which is then released at a certain moment and transforms consciousness."

In his book, Modern Man in Search of a Soul, Jungs states:

"The psyche is a self-regulating system that maintains itself in equilibrium as the body does. Every process that goes too far immediately and inevitable calls forth a compensatory activity."

There is a built-in mechanism of the soul-personality-ego-character-SOUL that puts into operation those invisible Soul Forces that will bring about the necessary correction of the ego when it gets too far out of control and does not willfully bring about its own correction. This is true of both the individual and the collective.

Exercise

Purpose: To demonstrate the cause – effect relationship of the choices, actions and consequences of the soul-personality-ego-character-**SOUL**.

Materials: A variety of demonstration materials can be obtained from mass media, case studies, myths, proverbs and other sources that demonstrate behavior out of control and having to be corrected by forces outside of the ego. The ego is but one aspect of the soul-personality-ego-character-SOUL.

Exercise 1:   Present the case material. Have group discuss the case example(s). The group can discuss or meditate on ways that the soul-personality-ego-character-**SOUL** could have corrected itself voluntarily so that it could have avoided the need to be corrected from without.

Each person in the group should give personal examples of symbolic incidences in their own growth wherein the correction had to be imposed from without rather than from within the soul-personality-ego-character-**SOUL**. Group feedback should be on ideas of strengthening the will power to make conscious, correct choices about growth and development.

The Law of Involution and Evolution

Gaskell defines this as the law of process of life, whereby the Spirit descends into matter and ascends therefrom.

The Law of the Earth

The I Ching defines this law as "alter the full and contribute to the modest."

The Law of Synchronicity

Jung employed this term to refer to meaningful co-incidences which could not be explained by known scientific laws. He referred to these incidences as "acausal" or beyond a known physical cause.

Synchronicity can most simply be defined as those meaningful incidences which "just happen from nowhere" and cannot be explained rationally or scientifically.

Synchronicity is the spontaneous coming together in time and space of symbols (words, events, etc) that make a meaningful connection between seemingly unrelated and unconnected happenings. It is the spontaneous interweaving and alignment of the outer world with the inner world.

Exercise

Purpose: To demonstrate the underlying inter-connectedness of the Soul.

1. The Soul is the Great Weaver that interweaves all of reality into one great whole.

> The group should be sensitized to look for and record synchronistic occurrences which happen during the week leading up to the group or even during the actual group experience. These are discussed during the group. The synchronistic experiences of the past that group members have experienced might also be discussed. Some of the situations which greatly enhance synchronistic experiences are birth, death, severe pain and illness, intense prayer, intense research, certain rituals, etc.

2. Sentence Completions:
   What does "being in synch" mean._____
   _____
   _____

   Give examples of incidences of when you felt "in synch"._____
   _____

   Give examples of synchronistic experiences that have happened to you. _____
   _____
   _____

   What are some of the ways to increase or enhance synchronistic possibility?_____

3. Associated Synthetic Learning, (ASL) Techniques The Law of Synchroniticy

The goal is to find common everyday occurrences in the life of the child to help the child concretely experience the working dynamics of each Law of The Soul. The operation of the Laws of the Soul are usually manifested in the unconscious background of our attitudes and behaviors until they are brought into the foreground of conscious awareness. In a culture or environment where the reality and existence of the Soul is denied, these background expressions of the Soul may never be brought into the conscious mind. Or they may be brought into the conscious mind too late to save it from some disaster that the "background expressions" were trying to save it against.

The purpose of helping children to understand their behavior-values-attitudes in the context of a Higher Being or intelligent "force-field", the Soul, that expresses itself in everyday life, is to help them to internalize a sense of Cultural Connectedness, Meaning, Purpose and Mission.

Once these basic Laws Of The Soul are taught, they can be associated to many other areas of the child's, parent's, family's and community's life and interactions.

4. law Of Synchronicity

Write a paragraph on your understanding of the law of synchronicity. _____
_____
_____
_____

_____
_____
_____
_____
_____
_____
_____
_____
_____
_____
_____
_____
_____
_____
_____
_____
_____
_____
_____
_____
_____
_____

5. Trigger Questions On Synchronicity

When things are in "synch.", what can one expect?
When things are out of "synch", what can one expect?
How do the following categories increase their "synch" value
    or energy?_____

_____

1.   Individual
2.   Family
3.   Community
4.   Cultural groups

Can "synch" be expressed between people and non-humans, for example animals?

Can "synch" be expressed between people and things like trees, rocks, the ocean, etc.

The Law of Centroversion

A law described by E. Neuman which defines the tendency of all systems to seek balance by returning to the center.

The Law of Eternal Change

"There is nothing more constant than change." Chance can be viewed as occurring simultaneously in three realms:

1. **Changeless Change**—The realm of the Perfect; that which is eternal and never changes yet is the hub of all changes.
2. **Serial Change**—Change occurring in cycles—circadian cycles of menstruation, sleep, gestation, hormonal cycles and their relations to cosmic cycles of moon and sun.
3. **Sequential Change**—the realm of rational-logical-ordered changes brought about by the intervention of the human will.

Soul-Centered Cultural Habit Training
(Cultural Attitude-Value-Behavioral Traits/Habits)

The Goal of Cultural Schema (Habits/Traits) Training is:

1. To apply the Laws Of The Soul to practical everyday maturation of the soul-personality-ego-character-SOUL at the physical, emotional, mental and spiritual levels of development.
2. To develop cultural self awareness and awareness of interpersonal dynamics and transactions within a cultural, Soul-Centered context.

3. To instill awareness of, and to effectuate change, through the laws of cause and effect (Karma)-the central law of the Soul.
4. To help each individual develop a strategy for learning concepts that arises from his/her behavior and interactions with the environment especially as it relates to Soul-Centered cultural development.
5. To help individuals to develop the ability to:

   a. Conceptualize—know the definition and characteristics of a concept.
   b. Abstract at more than one level at the same time.
   c. learn to learn

6. To help develop Soul-Centered values such as endurance, persistence, perseverance, integrity and transcendence through helping the person make more spiritual-rational choices, making decisions and acting to bring about change.
7. To help undo the Negative Self Concept by instilling Hope and Faith which serve as the stimulus for the creative generative force necessary for our survival.

FOR NOTES
Insights, Reflections, Self-Observations

Chapter 14:

Soul Force Integrative Exercises For Family/Community Development

NTU

NTU is the essence of Vital force or Soul Force. It is the central cohesive energy which is the centripetal force of TRUTH that draws all things back to the "Source," the "Origin," the "Center", the "Heart", the "Self." Ntu is the Heart around which a unified view of the Whole is spun. It is the core reality which is the survival instinct and the urge to Re-Union. It is the still, quiet voice of conscience that urges us upward towards perfection and into the inner "Community of Oneness."

NTU is the First, Efficient, and Final cause of all that is, has been and will be. It is a **building unit of Spiritual-Human Life**, it is a power and relation to inner TRUTH, and the "Rightness of Things (Ma-at)".

In West African, Bantu tradition, ntu is a root word that is the nucleus of the spiritual laws governing the relationships between people, animals, things, time, space and other modalities such as beauty, truth and justice.

All energies have a basic unit. The basic unit of electricity is the ohm. The basic unit of Soul Force could be considered as the ntu according to Bantu philosophy.

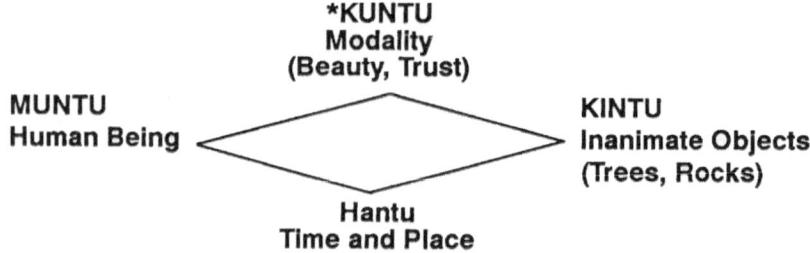

*KUNTU
Modality
(Beauty, Trust)

MUNTU
Human Being

KINTU
Inanimate Objects
(Trees, Rocks)

Hantu
Time and Place

***The above diagram is taken from the book entitled Mantu,
page 114 by Janheinz Jahn.**

NTU, in the Bantu African tradition, parallels the concept of rtu in Hindu cosmology and chi in Taoism. Rtu, chi and ntu refer to the established realm of Law and Order which prescribes Destiny, Sacred Customs, Regulation, Right Relation, Truth and Right Direction. Ntu then is the seed energy for the whole world and cosmos. It is the Center of right relationships between people, things, animals, colors, music, joy, sadness, ancestral spirits, and natural forces. Rivers flow in obedience to ntu and the crimson dawn is set ablaze by ntu, so "under the harness of ntu" a sacrifice is kindled necessitating the choice of surrender and alignment to these ever-present, ever-emergent paradigms of human consciousness.

Today these paradigms of human consciousness are being referred to in science as the "re-emergent Dark Feminine"-the archetypal symbol of the Soul, the Primal Shadow. The Orisha-Archetypal-Soul Forces of the unconscious mind are guardians of ntu. Ntu is the creative, karmic, primal heat of the SOUL. It is the Mother of all things. Ntu is the creative process at the Heart or Center of the Mandala of Self that begets and brings forth from the beginning unto the end-which is reflected in, and caught up in, the beginning. Ntu is the **self renewing**, transcending course that is fixed and invariable from the beginning to the end of time. It is the path of our destiny and the law of our being. Ntu stretches out into manifestation through patterns, tendencies and attractions, all of which clumped together would be called schema. Ntu is therefore the basic **energy unit** of the schema or imago-templates. The environmental (outer context) and personality-character (internal context) schema are ways or patterns to get things organized, ways of getting things done, ways of storage and retrieval of information. These schema are patterns of problem solving behaviors, patterns of relationships and relating.

Ntu is the healing model for growth in the new era. Participation in the Soul Centered Community Circle can be a healing/growth process that will help one to find the true process of growth/healing within oneself. This is done through a process of reciprocation: The Soul Centered Community Circle empowers one through its gifts of sharing and participation in collective knowledge. In return, one empowers the Circle's mission, by giving back, of one's knowledge, gifts, Truth and Soul Force energies that draw all things back to the Source, the "Origin", the "Heart", The Self".

This process of growth-maturation-healing will then enable the Soul-Centered Community Circle to administer to the individual, the family and the community, to the world, and the universe. The soul-personality-ego-character-SOUL in it's true I-dentity is the moving force, and integral nucleus at the Heart and center of this universal healing process. This happens through participation, input and witnessing.

Soul-Personality-Ego-Character-SOUL
and the Seven-Leveled World of Desire and Ntu Experience

The soul-personality-ego-character-SOUL is a process of cyclical dynamic life wherein that which has been separated from the Source of Oneness and Unity—the inner Beloved Community—strives to find the path of Self-Discovery and Re-Union. The soul-personality-ego-character-SOUL struggles to re-I-dentify, to re-unite with this Heart, the Center—the Source, the SOUL, the BA, the SAHU (the divine indwelling SELF of the ancient Egyptians).

The total movement—out from the Source and the Return To The Source, constitutes the circle, the wheel, or the Mandala of the Journey INTO THE SELF. The path of this journey can be symbolized as the journey of the soul-personality-ego-character seeking SELF-SOUL.

The soul-personality-ego-character-SOUL is the archetype of synthesis, individuation and initiation. It therefore is responsible as coordinator for balance, harmony and Self-Realization in the developmental process. From its germinal seed-form, it evolves and grows through the seven value-emotional-behavioral-attitudinal spiritual energy levels of the Soul and world. (These seven levels have been previously outlined and are listed again below). The soul-personality-ego-character-SOUL integrates all of the various manifestations of ntu energy.

The soul-personality-ego-character-SOUL consists of two opposite energies seeking balance, namely the Shadow (primal dark and the false dark) and the Light. These two opposite energies comprise what could be called a **central-organizing nucleus**. This central organizing (coordinating) nucleus is variously spoken of in different cultures as the **Indweller** and other similar names. In Yoruba culture of west Africa, it is called Ori, in Tahitian culture it is called Oro, in ancient Egyptian culture is was called Khu. Each of the concepts of the various cultures consists of a lower and a higher aspect to express the two opposite energies seeking balance.

A similar concept in Western tradition would be the Christ and in Eastern tradition would be the Buddha. The soul-personality-ego-character must travel through the universal symbolic "fields" of human-divine experience in order to internalize and integrate the various symbols of Self-Mastery, Self-Control and Self-Transcendence and thus unfold the Indweller. The below diagram outlines some of the characteristics of the universal imago –template fields of symbolic experiences that a person must travel through during the growth-maturational process regardless of culture or ethnic background.

As the soul-personality-ego-character-SOUL grows through these symbolic, life-experience levels, it interacts with, and through, four manifested aspects of energy. All of these manifested aspects of energy have, according to Bantu philosophy, as a rule, the root letters ntu—as outlined previously. They are Muntu, Kuntu, Hantu and Kintu. The soul-personality-ego-character must re-establish a truthful relationship to these different manifestations of energy, thus unfolding the SOUL or Indweller.

Each of the seven symbolic life-experience levels has its own characteristic vibrational pattern of ntu energy even though each participates in all of the other types of energies. Each level has its correspondences in the various manifestations of Nature and the cosmos. Therefore each level has its plants, animals, gemstones, planet, color, music notes that correspond pretty much across cultures.

VIOLET

Pineal Charkra — **Transcendent And Cosmic Consciousness Center**
Ori—Emi—Olodumare
(Hero-Ori-Christ-Buddha Goddess)
(God(dess) Indwelling In The SELF)
(The Process Of Becoming One With God(dess))
(God(dess) Indewelling In Nature and Cosmos)
(The Ba Of The Ancient Egyptians)

PURPLE

Pituitary Charkra — **Intuitional-Cosmic Representational Center**
Third Eye
Inner Sight—(World Tree)

BLUE

Throat Charkra — **Synesthesia And Inner-Mastery Center**
(Death-Rebirth-Beauty-Truth)
(Manifestation Center)
(Cornucopia Center)

GREEN

Heart Charkra — **Love And Surrender Center**
Heart—Love-Healing-Alignment

YELLOW

Navel Charkra — **Choice And Power Center**
Masculine-Father-Will power-Solar Plexus

ORANGE

Genital Charkra   **Emotions And Sensation Center**
Feminine-Mother-Generatiavity-Nurturance

RED

Basal Charkra   **Symbiotic, Sympathetic, Security Center**
Child-Trickster-Path finder-Fool-Opener of
the Way (Rebellion Center)

As the soul-personality-ego-character-SOUL grows through the various symbolic life-experiences of the different levels, it collects information from each level. The information and the experiences from the seven levels are ultimately synthesized and integrated into a coherent sense of SELF—a United Field of Energy which constitutes COMMUNITY. Each of the seven levels consists of desired responses and attitudinal-value-behavioral responses (Ka bodies/affects).

In its growth through these various fields of ntu-experiences, the soul-personality-character has to internalize, actualize, realize and become-one-with (unite with-submit to-return to) certain universal laws, values and principles of the SOUL-SPIRIT that govern growth, maturation, initiation and transcendence.

FOR NOTES
Insights, Reflections, Self-Observations

FOR NOTES
Insights, Reflections, Self-Observations

CHAPTER 15:

The Return to the Heart-The Return to the Mother

It is time for a change—The Soul has sent out a call from its deep center or Heart for the "Return to the Source." The Mandala Soul Centered-ntu Healing Approach is designed to facilitate this change. The Soul Centered-ntu Approach recognizes that we are each a mandala, and like the Mandala which symbolizes the magic circle

Harmony

of the Self, we operate on many different levels of inter-relationships, within and without. We experience and grow on many levels at one time.

The Mandala Soul Centered-ntu Healing Approach also recognizes that, at one or more of these inner levels, the repressed soulful worldview of African people remains intact today as a unified system of beliefs, ideas, and practices. This repressed, yet intact, worldview has nurtured and sustained us from the Ground of consciousness down through the years. Even though we were forced to leave our soulful worldview, it never left us. Today, this soulful worldview is just as viable a representational system as ever before and we are spontaneously being re-introduced or initiated back into its symbols and energies.

From deep within the Souls of Black people and the world, this ancient invisible order of the Soul as Dark Mother is pushing its way through into consciousness, as symbolized in the Beloved Community of Martin Luther King, Jr. The re-emerging Dark Mother is Mother Nature and demands our alignment with the cosmic, harmonious cycles of growth and maturation which are built into nature and the universe. The return or the re-emergence of the Black Feminine, an inner spiritual force of balance, is razing the old, making way for the new. The Call of Return will insure that in this decade, the missing element, Black representation – the Soul of Mother Africa as a legitimate spiritual-intuitive worldview will be put into place.

To help facilitate this transition back into a harmonious relationships with the inner, natural and ancestral forces of the Soul and spiritual world of God, we have evolved the Mandala Soul Centered-ntu Healing process. This Soul-Centered Healing process is a Passage-Rites/Initiation process into personal and cultural development and maturation. A structured component of this for youngsters and their mentors is the Mandala Maturation Network. This is a rites-of-passage process for youth and will be explained in one of the future books of the Soul-Centered Series.

Mandala Soul Centered-ntu therapy is a self-healing process involving self observation, introspection, prayer, self-criticims, self-analysis meditation, visualization, and ritual. It depends on the daily exercise of spiritual unfoldment and growth through revelation, service, love, teaching, diet, exercise and practice of right relationships to Self and others. The object of Mandala-Soul Centered-ntu Healing is to develop a way of life that guides one's daily living and serves as the foundation of one's thoughts, actions, and deeds. This foundation goes beyond a mere religion, philosophy or belief and constitutes a way of life—the very essence of one's Being. It serves as the transformative principle of one's physical, emotional, mental and moral-spiritual attitudes and behavior.

The Return As A Rites of Passage

All initiation-rites of passage and maturational processes of Self development are designed to allow one to center oneself in the group mind/Soul and find the inner pathway of Transcendence.

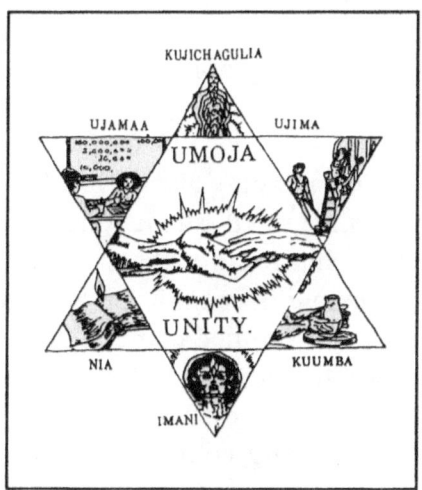

The Mandala of Community

Transcendence refers to the act of "going beyond" one stage of growth to the next higher stage of growth. Transcendence is an act of going beyond what sometimes seems like insurmountable barriers and impossible problems in development to find a peaceful, creative and growth-oriented solution.

The ability to go within and come back out with a renewed energy-to go beyond – is unique to the **transcendent-spiritual element** of the Africentric Soul-centered worldview, religion and culture. This unique **transcendental** quality of spirit which W.E. Dubois described as the "**gift of Black Folk**" allows us to develop through initiation and dialogue, a new sense of **altruistic_duty**. This new sense of duty would include a sense of **responsibility, commitment** and **right action** directed not towards the selfish self but towards the Collective Community, the Group Self or Soul.

> **Altruistic Selfless duty** means duty for the common good— whether that whole is seen as the family, extended family community, race, ethnic/national group, Mother Nature or the cosmos.

> **Selfish duty**_ -duty done in the expectation of winning someone's favor, getting into someone's good graces and in general getting something in return.

> **Self-Centered Duty** – duty done only to further one's personal cause.

The performance of one's duty always involves sacrifice, tension and even suffering for the growth and maturational process.

Psychological-moral Tension brought about through creative crisis is necessary for change and growth of the Soul and the inner Soul Forces. Out of tension and conflict, come the necessary ingredients of the process of change and growth. Without this necessary tension, avoidance of responsibility and diffusion of energy resources occur at all levels – individual, family, community and nation. Tension and creative conflict is necessary to push people beyond themselves and into new, often unexplored possibilities.

As the individual/group struggles through the different trials and tests of development, certain values and life-track themes are internalized and incorporated in the soul-personality-ego-character-SOUL.

The following ntu-soul-personality-ego-character-SOUL traits have been functionally evolved down through time within the Africentric Self-representational context. These have been necessary for the survival, development and stability of cultural self-esteem, self-image and sense of I-dentity. Some of these traits are:

a. strong sense of extended familyship and community

b. strong achievement and work orientation
c. adaptability of social roles
d. strong transcendental moral – spiritual orientation
e. strong affinity for, and utilization of, the intuitive, natural mode (gut feelings) of cognition

The following ntu-values have been central to the development of the Africentric soul-personality-ego-character-SOUL.

* collective work and responsibility (Ujima and Ujamaa)
* correct purpose (Nia)
* creativity (Kuumba)
* self determination

non-possession, selfless actions (sharing of goods, materials, time and resources)
respect for the Soul/innerself and the natural Soul Forces
charity and service to the less fortunate
perseverance and transcendence
understanding
faith
duty to one's mission in life
closure or putting things in correct relationship (MA-AT)**

*Principles of Kwaanza as espoused by Ron Karanga
**MA-AT – The Egyptian Goddess of right – relations, balance and world order. Her masculine aspect being the God Thoth the God of Knowledge and Wisdom.

In returning to the Source "Mother Africa Within", we must define the Group Soul – the Group Spirit, the Life-Track of the group. We must understand its characteristics, its dynamics, how it relates to us and how we relate to it. We must learn to empower it so that it can empower us.

Some of the empowering central cultural Life-Track ntu-Themes (symbolic-Energy Complexes) of the Soul-Centered worldview are:

Soul
Vital Force (Soul Force)
Orisha (Natural Forces)-Neters-Archetypes
Ancestral Veneration
Indweller
soul-personality-ego—character-SOUL
Zamani (past Perfect Time) (Great Time)—sasa (present time)
Purpose-Mission
Transcendence
Reincarnation-transmigration-transmutation
Intuition and Inner Guidance
Collective Soul (mind)—Group Soul (mind)

The Group Soul

Learn to symbolize these key concepts in creative ways through writing, poetry, music, art and other expressions.

Universal Principles of NTU*

This process of submission and uniting with the Life-Track of the InnerSelf and its principles is a process of "Centering" and it includes the internalization of symbols and values of Self-Control, Self-Mastery, Self-Realization and Self-Transcendence.

Some of the principles and Laws which regulate the growth and life of the Innerself-SOUL are:

1. Ahimsa (Hindu) or non-violence
2. Truth or non-lying
3. Imani—faith *
4. Closure or putting things in correct order according to Truth
5. Dharma (Buddhist)—duty to one's mission in life
6. Respect for the Mother—Feminine—generative power
7. Service to the elderly and the poor—Sara (Yoruba)
8. Control of the palate (correct diet and eating practices)
9. Collective work and responsibility and correct economics (Ujima and Ujamaa) *
10. Correct purpose (Nia) *
11. Creativity (Kuumba) *
12. Self-Determination (Kujichagulia) *
13. Chastity and correct use of sexuality
14. Non-possession, Selflessness (sharing of material goods)
    * Principle sof Kwaanza by Ron Karanga

NTU Generativity

Ntu-generativity is the generation of Soul Force – the force necessary to bring about change. Ntu-Soul Force generation is a philosophy of Work, Responsibility, Self-Determination, Family and Community Work. Ntu-Soul Force generation represents the collective effort necessary to bring about change and to create a new reality of Spiritual-Humanism. Through work, we generate a certain energy of unity, purpose and dedication known as Soul Force. The generation of Soul Force is vital to self and community development because it is the energy necessary to bring reality from the unmanifested to the manifested realm.

The Return of Unity

Soul Force is a energy force and like all energy forces, it has the potential to accomplish work and move things from one level of manifestation to another level. All things exist somewhere in the range between ideas and reality. Work is required to move them from the realm of ideas and into reality.

All material things eventually decay and fade back into the realm of ideas, memories and Spirit – the Collective SOUL. The Collective Soul Force, also known as the "Group Soul", is a result of the accumulation and contribution from a variety of Mandala-imago-symbolic-Energy-Soul Forces. These inner Soul Forces are intelligent forces of the soul-personality-ego-character-SOUL and they go beyond current concepts of ego psychology. These inner Soul Forces are variously referred to as complexes, archetypes, metaphors and symbols. They require recognition and development in the human psychic structure. In the African and eastern traditions, they are variously called spiritual forces, orisha, neters, gods. elohim, etc. They are a part of, as well as being housed in what Carl Jung would refer to as the collective unconscious mind. They are kept in harmony and in Community by a host of Universal and Eternal Laws—the central of which is karma.

These universal, symbolic forces and contents of the inner Self which guide and represent various "life experiences" need be, and must be, integrated in the conscious life of the individual and group. These inner Soul Forces influence and direct behavior from the recent and the archaic past. There are culturally preserved techniques and rituals of integrating these forces into conscious life. All cultures have some understanding at the overt and/or covert level of Spiritual Laws as opposed to man-made law. The Spiritual Laws provide for everything that could arise between man and God; man and Spirit, man and animal, plant and mineral world; man and modalities such as beauty, trust, love, righteousness, laugher, joy, etc.

NTU The Evolvement of the Spiritual-Rational Through Passive-Reflective Resistance and Direct Action.

It is in and through the "Soul" and Energy of Soul Force that we create, enliven our images, symbols, concepts and worldview. We empower a Human Spiritual-Rational representational system to guide our Souls, as well as the souls of others, towards a greater appreciation of the beauty, practicality and "aliveness" of the Rational-Spiritual Aesthetic—the beauty of Mother Nature in all of her aspects. Through developing this aesthetic we develop an awareness of the Inner Community of Oneness. The Central Coordinating Nucleus is but a door, a symbol which points beyond itself in the direction of creation, generativity, improvement and Self-Realization.

It is through generativity that we generate the necessary Soul Force Energy to bring things from the semi-real realm of concepts and images into the Real-Realm of Spiritual-Material Reality.

Further it is through generativity that we extend our image and symbol into the Cultural, Existential, Transcendental, Transpersonal, Spiritual, and Eternal realms of Self-Perpetuation and Self-Realization.

The Force Fields of Consciousness

Life is a force field composed of forces and opposing forces.

Every living being and non-living thing on this planet are being bombarded by a variety of impinging forces and is either applying sufficiently powerful opposing forces to remain stable, sustain growth, transcend the various maturational stages or is applying an insufficient opposing force and so is failing at life. For example:

The person who is ill is applying the opposing force of medication or the applied advice of a physician.

The student in school is applying the opposing force of active study to enlighten his/her areas of unknowing.

The employee is receiving the impinging force of having a job to do and is applying the opposing force of doing the job.

Many welfare recipients are receiving the negative impinging force of lack of money. They may be applying the reverse opposing force of spending less, or the positive opposing force of working an undisclosed job.

Life's pressures are impinging forces or stressors. At the point which a force is pressuring the central coordinating nucleus, an equal and opposing force must be applied to stabilize growth, maturation and transcendence. One must apply a greater and opposite force in order to overcome and grow or must suffer collapse and failure if less than equal opposing force is applied.

An important word which keeps cropping up is this "opposite". The more accurately focused the opposing force is, the less pressure will have to be applied to overcome it. That is to say, you want to attack the actual source of the problem, or as close to the source as possible, in order to be optimally effective.

To illustrate the meaning of this, let's take the first example. If the person who has an illness (e.g. Flu) takes medicine to cure the symptoms (e.g., runny nose) instead of medicine to cure the actual illness, he is not applying force to the source. If he takes more than the recommended dosage for the symptoms, thinking that this surely will cure his illness, he is increasing the force but is still not applying it directly to the source, and consequently, may get to a point where he feels better for a period of time, but may never be cured and may even die..

In the second example- the case of a student faced with the pressure of a physiology course he doesn't do well in – if he studies the material not realizing that cell structure is his problem area, he will have to study longer and harder in order to learn physiology than if he goes straight to the section on cell structure first. Conversely, if a student knows he has trouble with physiology, the correct method of overcoming it is to:

1. identify the specific area that he doesn't understand (Passive Reflection and Resistance through the halting effects of Consciousness.)
2. applying the opposing force there (Direct action which is this case would be study.)

It will then require less effort on his part and the study time he invests will be more productive.

From the above examples it can be seen that no matter how great the opposing force, it must be applied at the root of the problem in order to be most effective. Therefore the first step in solving a problem or combatting pressure is identifying the source. Consequently, the employee must initially apply himself to the specific tasks required of his position. In this way he will be most effective in that position and therefore be prepared to accept a promotion once his initial duties are mastered and it is obvious that he can handle more responsibility. Similarly, the individual with financial problems must identify the source of his monetary problem before he can effectively apply force and overcome it. Money is never the actual source of a problem. Perhaps it is the oppressive unfairness of racism and sexism. Perhaps it is an inability to work, inability to manage money, lack of knowledge, lack of a marketable skill, lack of desire to work, lack of self-confidence, ignorance of the job market, or any number of hindrances. Lack of money is only an indicator that some specific area of your life is not being (perhaps not able to be) effectively handled at that time.

Life's pressures have a purpose, they serve to strengthen our abilities, our talents, ourselves through Creative-Transcendence.

They serve to fortify positions that we already hold and they are the basis of mental, physical, ethical, social and spiritual growth.

Below is a table to illustrate how this works. The applications of this data to everyday life are infinite and will always be effective as long as we can first identify the real source of the pressure.

Impinging Force Pressure)	Opposing Force (Effort)	Result
x ntu units force	x ntu units force	stability, no movement, no growth
xx ntu units force	x ntu units force	failure, loss of ground
x ntu units force	xx ntu units force	growth, gaining of ground, progress, improvement

FOR NOTES
Insights, Reflections, Self-Observations

FOR NOTES
Insights, Reflections, Self-Observations

CHAPTER 16:

The Work Of Generating Ntu Force Within A Mandala Soul – Centered Community Circle

Each activity of change and creation that you undertake will be generating NTU units as you work. You may increase the force and energy of the NTU by blessing yourself, your work and the space in which you are working by inner thought and image, which you will hold in your mind while you work. "In the name of God (Olofi), my Innerself and Ancestors, I work so that I may grow in strength and give strength to others".

The Nurturant Mother

During the work of change, growth and creation is a time to make internal commitments to take responsibility for Self, yet at the same time be respectful to the needs of the Cultural Group as a whole.

The work of change, growth and creation is a time of "Being Here NOW". There is no other time for independence, liberation and self-development than the here and NOW.

During the Soul Force work of change, of growth and creation is an excellent time to allow one's Self to get Lost In The Moment. This frees up the control of the conscious mind and allows intuition to become the inner guide towards creative individual/Group Growth. It is an excellent time to learn new skills and symbolize with the new ntu energy. It is an excellent time to learn new patterns of inner organization, perception and problem solving.

The generation of NTU units of Soul Force is a time to go beyond the usual boundaries of the individual self to realize the right relationships to the Cultural Self. During this time we depend upon an internal value system of exchange called teh CAS = H System. (Caring And Sharing equals Humanity).

Ntu units are equal to and are transferable into CAS = H exchangeable units. Caring and sharing generates a type of energy which can be used for individual and Group Growth which, in this context, we will refer to as "Community".

The Soul-Force CAS = H System is established on the extended family network of supportive energy. It is designed to develop a pool of spiritual energy that can be used by the group and its members as a unit to help bring the unmanifested into the realm of the manifested.

Ntu-CAS = H leads to Right Power. The Circle unbroken is a Circle of Power Relationships. The Manddala ntu-CAS = H experience is one of shifting paradigms or shifting frames of reference and relationships. Ntu-CAS = H is an attempt to revitalize a worldview of Right Relationships and Right Power which both results from, and which helps to shape, shared Cultural Experiences. Ntu-CAS = H is an attempt to focus from cash as the end goal of attainment to CAS = H as the end goal. Here the process is seen as the product. Right Power then, is the proper understanding and utilization of NTU as Soul Force within the ntu-CAS = H system.

Right Power is one of recycling of energy within a Community of Shared Values and Beliefs. If we take and do not give back to the Community, not only does the energy that we have received become stagnant but also we as receivers become stagnant.

Humans, like all of life, are open systems and growth depends upon a give and take or a passage rather than a fixed state of remaining the same. CAS = H as a system of Right Power involves a change of consciousness, a transformation from a state of individual isolation and fragmentation to a state of unity and mutual support. CAS = H as a system of Right-Relations, Right-Power and Spiritual-Humanism, involves an initiation into deeper and deeper levels of self-consciousness as we move through the seven levels of emotional-behavioral-attitudinal growth.

Ntu-CAS = H as a system of Spiritual Humanism is considered one of the basic and more central aspects of Self-Empowerment and Self-Realization. If each member in the Mandala Soul-Centered Community Circle concentrates on actualizing some aspect of ntu-CAS = H system daily, weekly, monthly and yearly, the pool of energy will grow and become stronger.

Through the ntu-CAS = H system, we establish right power and right relations with our extended cultural family network and we awaken the presence of "Beloved Community" spoken of so often by Martin Luther King, Jr. This extended network of close personal relationships, images, symbols and values is an open system capable of endless reordering and transforming itself. The Soul-Centered Community Circle as a ntu-CAS = H system is designed as a means to help people fight against the growing feelings of alienation by participating in collective work to enhance the Self and Group.

In this extended family-Community Circle of ntu-CAS = H energy, each member is seen as the Center through which meaning, purpose, importance and power is interpreted. Networks are Self-Generating, Self-Organizing, and Self-Perpetuating Systems. The Mandala Soul-Centered Network, as such, is focused on renewal, empowerment, re-definition, I-dentity, motivation, rehabilitation, Self-Realization and Transcendence.

The Soul-Centered Community Circle is also a time of developing consciousness (of the Cultural Mind/SOUL), a consciousness of independence. Self-determination may be started in many ways but is completed only during the course of the actual struggle to maintain and sustain a Self-supporting, Self-functioning entity. In the growth process, the personal and the collective must mature through the seven levels properly, each must encounter the various experiences of the seven-leveled world both at the individual and the collective levels. According to Cabral, Self-determination requires the daily contact of the Self with the popular masses in the community. Self-determination then is a working integrative contact of the individual self with the Collective Self.

FOR NOTES
Insights, Reflections, Self-Observations

FOR NOTES
Insights, Reflections, Self-Observations

CHAPTER 17:

NTU-CAS = H Exchange A Soul-Centered Beloved Community Circle Unbroken

The Growing Ntu/CAS = H Exchange

The below outline of ntu-cash exchange units is intended to only serve as an example of how this has been adapted to fit the needs of a particular group of people serving to build a network of energy exchange in a particular period of its growth process. This outline is easily modifiable to other situations and institutions.

In order to receive you must first give. Do not receive without giving, otherwise the energy becomes stagnant and the receiver becomes stagnant.

Ways Of Giving	ntu Units	Cash = h
1. Counseling	20	20
2. Group Facilitator	10	10
3. Lecture and Workshop	20	20
4. Art	10-20	10-20
5. Graphic Arts	5	5
6. Alter Work	5	5
7. Public Relations	5	5
8. Workshop Helpers	N.E.	N.E.

9. Clerical Work	10	10
10. Cleaning	8	8
11. Decorating	5	5
12. Gardening	5	5

N.E. Stands for Non-Exchangeable units. This means that you cannot receive counseling services, but you can use the categories to become involved with other Center/group projects and services. The exchangeable units are varied. They can be used in exchange for counseling, Bach Flower Remedies, workshops, lectures and other services.

The CAS = H pool of spiritual energy of (NTU) is the evolving Group SELF, Group Soul or Transcendent Community. The SELF-SOUL is eternally vigilant and cannot be deceived. The SELF-SOUL is the KNOWER behind the known. It watches every act, word, deed, thought and gesture. It never sleeps and does not fatigue. It is an intelligent-symbolic network of energy. In order to keep it working constructively on our behalf in the maturational process, we must give attention to its cultivation. Anytime we take anything out of the system, we should put back something equal or greater in energy value.

This pool of energy has been helpful in the past in several ways in community building:

A. Common Cultural-Spiritual Bonding.
    1. The unmanifested realm where energy is used to bind members of the group together around an evolving, common, cultural value frame of reference, relating to the African-American, African-Caribbean ethic.
    2. The manifested realm wherein various needs have been serviced within and without the Circle such as the need for clothing, shelter, skills, money, contacts, equipment, etc.

This ntu-CAS = H pool of energy is the result of commitment, sacrifice, planning and most of all, action. The action is in the form of productive work. Productive work is work through which we grow.

Work that produces a product that has a value-context. A product cannot have a value context unless it is the result of the combined forces that participate within that value-context.

Cash in its standard monetary, materialistic sense is object oriented and is embedded in a value system of power-lust, and greed. CAS = H in the Mandala Soul-Centered sense is Essence oriented and is embedded in the Tree of Universal Values and Ancestral Cultural Beliefs.

CAS = H is a system of mutual giving to all those involved in its system. Synergy is the bonus energy resulting from harmonious interactions within the CAS = H SYSTEM. Synergy is expressed and felt when more work is done with less energy and when things just naturally fit into place. CAS = H represents a shift in attitudes and consciousness from an individual, material focus to a decentralized, cooperative enterprising network.

B. Ways of taking Soul Force or NTU energy units away from Self-Community Development:

Not giving back full and in good spirit.
Holding personal inner resentments because one has to share.

Ways of putting Soul Force or NTU Energy units back into Self-Community Development.

1. Commitment to sharing freely and in a loving spirit.
2. Helping others to overcome their resistance to and resentment of sharing and giving back.

Mandala Beloved Community Circle Unbroken

Ways Of Giving

-- Visiting the sick
-- Facilitating groups, lectures, workshops
-- Money donations
-- Goods, donations of clothing, books, plants, furnishings

-- Clerical work
-- Cleaning and decorating, gardening

Mandala Soul – Centered CAS = H Rewards

Child Rearing and Family Management.
The Seven Areas of Attitudinal-Value and Behavioral development.

The Soul or Invisible Moral Body, the Light and Consciousness body must be developed just as the other aspects of the body are developed.

Just as the physical body, emotional body, intellectual body grows and matures, the invisible body of the Soul must also be attended to in its correct growth. If the Soul is not attended to in its correct growth, certain aspects of the Soul will become undeveloped and lag in its maturation.

The undeveloped aspects of the Soul tend to act in an unhealthy and disruptive way in the growth of the soul-personality-ego-character-SOUL structure.

The SOUL, being the Indwelling Light of the body, tends to draw all aspects of the soul-personality-ego-character into the higher realm of Light. However, if the Indwelling Light is left undeveloped and in darkness, it tends to draw all aspects of the soul-personality-ego-character into darkness.

Soul-Centered-Healing has the purpose of helping the individual to develop consciousness of the Inner Light Body of the Soul. After consciousness of the Inner Light Body, Soul-Centered Healing is the act of shining this Light of Self-Consciousness into the undeveloped areas of the soul-personality-ego-character structure and assisting these areas of the Soul to move from the darkness into the Light. These undeveloped areas of the soul-personality-ego-character must be assisted into active development and growth, from disruption and disunity to harmonious Unity within the Self and Community.

Soul Force NTU-CAS = H System for Parenting
We Must Be Right in Our Actions and
Intentions (MA-AT) Marks of Maturity

Review of the Seven Areas of Attitudinal-Value-Behavioral Development (Age Grouping 9-14 or Younger). For parents and parent surrogates.

I.   Right Attitude—Home
1. Study—has right attitude of self-responsibility toward studying.
2. Relating to others—has right attitude of respect towards adults.
3. Relating to others—has right attitude of respect towards siblings, peers and others.
4. God, Prayer, Ancestors, Philosophy, Life, etc,--assumes some attitude of reflection, introspection, meditation, prayer during the week.
5. Relating to things—has right value of, and respect for, property (own and others.)

II. Personal Hygiene And Self-Care Functions—Home
1. Bathes self without assistance and/or reminders.
2. Right attitude towards self-hygiene.
3. Combs hair without assistance, to social satisfaction.
4. Brushes teeth without assistance on daily basis.
5. Participates in care of clothing (washing, ironing, etc.)

III. Chores—Home
1. Performs chores without having to be constantly reminded.
2. Takes on unassigned chores.
3. Thoroughness in completing chores. (Places everything back into proper order)
4. Chores performed with right attitude.
5. Completing chores in a timely manner.

IV. Learning Process—Home And School

1. School—goes to school without prompting or being forced.

2. Study—studies without constant urging (Homework)

3. School—academic attitudes/behaviors. (Keeps up with Classwork)

4. School—social-emotional attitudes/behaviors. (Behaves in school)

5. Has made the necessary preparations for going off to school in the mornings—i.e. – packing books, etc.

V.   Demonstration Of Proper Values

1.   Sharing
2.   Bravery
3.   Love
4.   Truth
5.   Harmony
6.   Creativity
7.   Nobility of Spirit
8.   Forgiveness
9.   Sense of Duty and Responsibility
10. Sense of Commitment
11. Prayer and Faith
12. Sacrifice
13. Unity
14. Creativity
15. Responsible Independence

The parents, and where applicable, also the counselors, therapists, teachers and other responsible role models are to enter points in the soul-personality-ego-character-SOUL Journal (The Black Book) each week along with their signatures.

It is possible to gain 54-66 ntu points total each week.

The youngster must have accumulated a designated percentage of the total ntu points at the time of award of privileges, gifts and closure celebration.

Extra "ntu" points may be gained in Area V—Demonstration of proper values.

The following two ntu-attitudinal-value-behavioral rating categories are designed for therapist who work with children at the individual and/or group level.

VI. Group Participation-Interactional Process

1. Respectful of authority of the group.
2. Contributes creatively to the group
3. Respectful of the rights of other members of the group.
4. Shares and helps other members of the group.
5. Respectful of the rules of the group.

    a. being on time for the group
    b. not disrupting the group
    c. concentrating on the lesson for the day (good concentration and attention)
    d. participating on closure of the group

VII. Individual-Therapeutic Interactional Process

1. Attendance and punctuality.
2. Cooperation and exchange.
3. Progress towards the achievement of attitudinal-value-behavioral (AVBA) assignment number 1._____

4. Progress towards the achievement of (AVBA) assignment number 2._____

5. Progress towards the achievement of (AVBA) assignment number 3._____

The attitudinal-value-behavioral assignments (ABVA) are based on the projected short and long term goals for the particular client being assessed. A rule of thumb, by no means set-in-stone, is that the therapeutic process should be focused on the accomplishment of about three goals at one particular phase of the therapeutic process. In the above category of Individual-Therapeutic-Interactional-Process, attitudinal-value-behavioral assignment (AVBA) numbers 1 and 2 should be monitored as short term goals and (AVBA) number 3 should be monitored as one of the targeted long term goals.

NTU-CAS = H Point System

Weekly total possible points:

54—Ntu without regular teacher input.
66—with regular teacher input.

Monthly total possible points:

216—Ntu points without regular teacher input.
265—Ntu points with regular teacher input

Toy Store (For Exchange of UTA-Points)

150 points toys

200 points toys

300 points toys

400 points toys

500 points toys

700 points toys

1000 points toys

FOR NOTES
Insights, Reflections, Self-Observations

FOR NOTES
Insights, Reflections, Self-Observations

CHAPTER 18:
Ntu-Soul Force Prayers and Affirmations

The prayers, affirmations and exercises appended herein are intended to serve only as seed-outlines for the creative generation of other ideas from within your own and group's Soul-Center.

For Boys and Girls

O Lord our God, who art everywhere present, teach us in home and school to serve one another and to conquer self. Give us thankful desires so that we may love and praise you always.

Inner Guidance

Help me Guardian—Ori, To Be
More and More, each day like thee
Enhance my awareness so that I might see
the SELF, the Truth, the Reality
that is greater than me
Unite me with my Family
Unite me with my Friends
Unite me with my Soul Force Brothers and Sisters
Unite me with my Ancestors

Soul Force Affirmation

I am not only human but I am Divine.
My Inner Self is an expression of my Divinity.
I must always seek to know and grow into the powers
of my Innerself.
I will seek to grow beyond the five senses to awaken
the SOUL FORCE, the magic, transformative energy of the
SELF. I will seek to enter the Beloved Community and move
beyond fragments of reality to the WHOLE.

What are the five senses?

1.
2.
3.
4.
5.

What is the Sixth Sense?
How does the Sixth Sense relate to the Soul-Innerself.
What are some of the powers of the InnerSelf or Soul?
What is Soul Force?
What is Divinity?
What is the Indweller and what are some of the names for it?

Adult's Affirmations To Develop (ori)—Soul Force

I know that it is Good, Right and Just that I give time and other resources to help the brothers and sisters who are less fortunate than myself.

I affirm that nothing can stop that which is Good, Right and Just for the common good of all from manifesting.

In order to best serve and grow, I must make the best use of my time during periods of progress and success, for these periods wax and wane like the cycles of the moon and ocean.

I affirm that I will make the most effective, efficient and productive use of time while involved in the work of the Inner Self.

In order to best develop my inner soul-character-ego-personality-SOUL and resources, and in order to best capitalize upon resources around me, I must pay attention and respect to the right times and places for things to be manifested.

I affirm that I will spend time developing my Center each day. I will dedicate, contemplate and pray. I will synchronize and harmonize my work to manifest with energies of the right time and the right place.

The Initiation Into Self

The Self has a hold on me, and won't let go.
It directs and guides me
and tells me so-and-so.
*It reveals me to me_*
And shows me things
I normally would not see.
It thinks for me in a higher mode.
It's always there to help carry the load.
It's a hidden and invisible Force.
A reflection of the God-Source.
It's the axis of the initiation change
It's the center of all that will be re-arranged.
It is the seed of my African Soul.
It draws me ever into the transformative mould.
It is the inner authority that requires submission
Through many a transition, and puts my fears,
weaknesses, anxieties into remission.
It is the Light and Energy of Creation,
It Empowers and Enlightens without cessation.

Prayer of Reverence to the Great Mother and the Dark Feminine

Hail Isis, Yemanya, Woyangi, Hathor, Mary, Ma-at, Sekmet and other Virgin Queens of the Universe. Hallowed be thy names as aspects of Divinity.

Sacred is the Light, thy Son, that shineth-forth from the darkness of thy Soul's womb as Horus/Christ/Ori. Most Holy Great Mothers, absorb us in thy Light and Being. Guide and direct us back to the Source and to reunion with thy Love and Grace.

FOR NOTES
Insights, Reflections, Self-Observations

FOR NOTES
Insights, Reflections, Self-Observations

REFERENCES BY CHAPTERS:

Chapter 1:

St. Augustine: The City Of God, Double Day,
New York, 1952.

Chapter 3:

Jung, Carl: Modern Man In Search of a Soul, New York,
Harvest Books, 1933.

Woodson, Carter G.:   The Mis-education of the Negro,
Associated Publishers, Washington, DC,
1933.

Chapter 5:

Conrad, Earl: The Invention of the Negro, Paul Eriksson,
Inc. New York, 1966.

Ellison, Ralph: The Invisible Man, Vintage Books, New
York, 1947.

Hauser, Stuart: Black and White Identity Formation. John
Wiley, New York, 1971.

Schreiber, Flora F.: Sybil, Warner Books, New York, 1973.

Thigpen, Corbett; The Three Faces of Eve, Augusta, Cleckley, Hervey: GA, 1985.

Chapter 6:

Bernal, Martin: Black Athena; The Afroasiatic Roots of Classical Civilization, Volume I: The Fabrication Of Ancient Greece 1785-1985, Rutgers University Press, New Brunswick, New Jersey, 1987.

King, Martin Luther   Where Do We Go From Here: Chaos or Community?. Beacon Press, Boston, 1967.

Morrison, Toni: Tar Baby, Signet Books, New York, 1981.

Chapter 7:

Goldberg, Philip: The Intuitive Edge-Understanding and Developing Intuition, Jeremy P. Tarcher, Inc. Los Angeles, Calif. 1988.

Hannah, Barbara: Encounters With The Soul—Active Imagination by C.G. JUNG, Sigo Press, 1981.

Chapter 8:

Brunton, Paul: The Spiritual Crisis Of Man, Samuel Weiser, Inc., York Beach, Maine, 1981.

Cirlot, J.E: Dictionary of Symbols, Philosophical Library New York, N.Y.

Gaskell, G.A.:   Dictionary Of All Scriptures & Myths, Julian Press, Inc. New York, N,Y, 1960.

Heaney, John: The Sacred And The Psychic; Parapsychology and Christian Theology, Paulist Press. New York, N.Y. 1984.

Henderson, Joseph: Thresholds Of Initiation, Wesleyan University Press, Middletown, Conn., 1967.

Schaer, Hans: Religion And The Cure Of The Soul In Jung's Psychology, Pantheon Books, New York, N.Y. 1950.

Wilhelm/Baynes: The I Ching: Or Book Of Changes, Princeton University Press, Bollingen Series XIX, 1977.

Chapter 14:

Janheinz, Jahn:.   Muntu, New African Culture, Grove Press, Inc. New York, 1961.

References—Dark Feminine And Soul As Feminine

Begg, Ean: The Cult Of The Black Virgin, Arkana, New York, 1985.

Bernal, Martin: Black Athena: The Afroasiatic Roots of Classical Civilization, Rutgers University Press, New Brunswick, New Jersey. 1987.

Birkhauser-Oeri, Sibylle: The Mother, Archetypal Image in Fairy Tales. Inner City Books, Toronto, Canada. 1988.

Cabrera, Lydia: Yemaya Y Ochun, C-R, Madrid, Spain. 1974.

Chapin-Massey, Marilyn: Feminine Soul: The Fate of an Ideal, Beacon Press, Boston, Massachusetts. 1985.

Neumann, Erich: Amor and Psyche: The Psychic Development of the Feminine, Princeton University Press, 1956.

"   "   The Great Mother: An Analysis Of The Archetype, Princeton University Press. 1955.

Perera, Sylvia B.: Descent to the Goddess: A Way of Initiation for Women, Inner City Books, Toronto, Canada, 1981.

Ponce, Charles: Working The Soul: Reflections on Jungian Psychology, North Atlantic Books, Berkeley, California. 1988.

Redgrove, Peter: The Black Goddess And The Unseen Real: Our Unconscious Senses And Their Uncommon Sense, Grove Press, New York, 1987.

Weaver, Rix: The Wise Old Woman: A Study Of Active Imagination, G.P. Putnam's Sons, New York, 1973.

Whitmont, Edward C.: Return of the Goddess, Crossroads, New York, 1982.

Supplimental Reading List

Arguelles, Jose & Miriam: Mandala, Berkeley, Calif, Shambala Publ. 1972.

Awolalu, Omosade: Yoruba Beliefs and Sacrificial Rites, Longman Group, Ltd., Essex UR, 1979.

Barrett, Leonard, E.: Soul Force: African Heritage in Afro-American Religion. Doubleday, New York, 1974.

Ben Jochannan, Y.: Africa: Mother-of Western Civilization. Alkebu-lan Books, New York, 1971.

"   "   African Origins of the Major Western Religions. Alkebu-lan Books, New York, 1970.

"   "   Black Man of the Nile. Alkebu-lan Books, New York, 1972.

Bennett, Lerone, Jr.: "The Lost Found Generation". Ebony, August, 1978.

Berg, Phillip: The Wheels Of A Soul, Research Centre Of Kabbalah, New York, 1984.

Bettleheim, Bruno: Freud and Man's Soul, Vintage Books, New York, 1982.

Bolling, John L.: The Changing Self-Concept of Black Children: The Black Identity Test, Journal of the National Medical Assoc., Jan., 1974.

Carrington, Hereward: The Coming Science, American Universities Publishing Co. New York, NY. 1920

Dourley, John: The Illness That We Are; A Jungian Critique of Christianity, Inner City Books, Toronto, Canada, 1984.

Groddeck, Georg: The Book of the It, New York: Vintage, 1949.

Grotjahn, Martin: The Voice of the Symbol, New York, Delta 1971.

Guidham, Arthur: The Psychic Dimensions Of Mental Health, Turnstone Press Limited, England, 1982.

Hauser, Stuart: Black and White Identity Formation. John Wiley, New York, 1971.

McClester, Cedric: Kwanzaa, Gumbs and Thomas Publishers, New York, 1985.

Toldson, I.:   Roots of Soul- The Psychology of Black Expressiveness, Anchor Press/Doubleday, Garden City, New York, 1982.

And

The Fork In The Road

Yvette, Samuel: The Choice: The Issue of Black Survival In America, Cottage Books, Silver Springs, Md. 1971

**We Are Down To The Choice
Chaos Or Community**

FOR NOTES
Insights, Reflections, Self-Observations

FOR NOTES
Insights, Reflections, Self-Observations

www.ingramcontent.com/pod-product-compliance
Lightning Source LLC
Chambersburg PA
CBHW061353280526
45784CB00001B/245